To Murray,

All The Best!

Larry

11-11-21

TAKEAWAYS

*101 Lessons from 30 Years
as a Silicon Valley CEO*

Lacy Edwards

TAKEAWAYS

*101 Lessons from 30 Years
as a Silicon Valley CEO*

TABLE OF CONTENTS

INTRODUCTION

After reaching the stage in my life when I had the opportunity to pause and look around, I asked myself *How did I end up here?* and *What have I learned along the way?* This book is a result of my attempts at answering those questions.

Takeaways is a compilation of lessons learned, aimed at sharing them with those who are interested and those who may benefit. Like most lessons in life, learning them on your own through experience is the most effective way, but unfortunately also the most time consuming and costly. By sharing my *Takeaways* with some examples, maybe you can relate well enough and apply as appropriate to your situation.

I spent twelve years in Silicon Valley in a variety of technology sales and management jobs before getting my first position as chief executive officer (CEO), a role that I was fortunate to fill with six companies for most of the following thirty years. With that appointment, the real learning started. Carrying the responsibility for the success of an entire company is weighty. It took me a few years in the role to recognize, understand, and fully appreciate that. The ego trip that comes with the CEO title diminishes when you start realizing the sheer number of challenges that must be dealt with every day. As you will see as you read this book, my style is to live by the phrase "Just net it out". I guess that's how I was able to pack thirty years of experience and learning into a book of this size.

Over the years, I spent many hours reflecting on what I was learning. I have always disliked using working hours sitting on an airplane, so for most long-distance flights I took the red-eye. Since I can't sleep on an airplane, that gave me ample time write down my thoughts, which were often short notes and single-sentence observations. In the late 1990s, when the BlackBerry craze began, that's what I started using to keep track of my thoughts. I started referring to them as my BlackBerry Philosophies.

That same BlackBerry Philosophy style is reflected in this book, which is get to the point, say what I want to say, stop talking, then move on. My editors were constantly urging me to give more descriptive stories and examples, and I always resisted. My response was, "The people I've written this book for don't need more examples or more detailed descriptions. They'll get it!"

As you can imagine, after thirty years of red-eye flights, the number of single-sentence observations built up. One of my challenges with this book was deciding which ones to include or, perhaps more accurately, which ones to leave out. So in an attempt to be interesting, relevant, and convey the most meaningful lessons, I chose what I felt were the most important and relevant 101 lessons.

Over the years, I am fortunate to have had the opportunity to work with and lead some amazing people and to learn many valuable lessons from them. To them I say "Thank you!"

Getting to share what they taught me with you is an honor and a privilege.

I hope you enjoy the book!

ACKNOWLEDGEMENTS

I realize acknowledging 200 people may be viewed as a little over-board. But in my case, without these 200 people this book would not exist. Also keep in mind, this book was written over a period of 30 years. So if I included everyone the number of acknowledgements would probably be closer to 500.

To really do justice for this section I would have to write another book. But at the risk of leaving out important people, I still must try to acknowledge some of those to whom I owe a tremendous amount of gratitude for their support, patience, education, and friendship during my career. Many of these names you will see multiple times. They are the ones who were willing to make multiple runs at success with me.

Those of us who spent our youths together learning and just trying to survive:

Margy Wall, Maxine Mitchell, Bill Rocha, Gary Lawrence, Christine Mederios, Nick Derdevanis, Fred Carlson, Judy Roth Kelso, Jack Riley, Russ Clark, Karen Wood, Chris Adams, Joan Kniskern, Eric Gnau, Joe Farrell, Cindy Taylor, Bob Hess, Chuck Hamilton

The XA Team:

Marc Fey, Les Murphy, Rick Armstrong, Kent Jarvi, Tom McHugh, Joanne Markham, Pat Neisen, Richard Vincent, Joe Broderick, Tom Seifert, John Figliulio, Julie Lane, Ed Mott, Steve Kehaya, Paul Buckley, Patricia Foerster, Phil Sheridan, Karen Wood, Jodie Tatro, Mike Grimm, Tom Michael, Mary Barowski, Jim Sutton, Zad Roumaya, Hollis Graves, Dan Grant, Greg Amariti, Jerry Orris, Bob Kagle, Bill Kaiser, Pari DeSorbay, Jim Hildner, Rich Graham

The Unison Team:

Don Lee, Mike Casteel, John Ferraro, Gwynn Rachlin, Tanya Candia, Phil Sheridan, Patricia Foerster, Julie Lane, Zad Roumaya, Dick Skuse, Steve Danseglio, Karen Wood, Richard Heal

The Evoke Team:

Julie Lane, Jack Olson, Carl Zeigler, Joe Farrell, John Giglio, Kathryn Hewetson, Katie Dalessandro, Seth Lieber, Irwin Lieber, Larry Wagenberg, Cristina Morgan, Jim Robinson III, Jim Robinson IV, Stuart Ellman, Bob Forlenza, Eckhard Bogner, Andy Galewsky, Jeff Millman, Mario Gamez, Art Demaio, Chris Buckley, Pari DeSorbay , Dave Shewmake, Don Townsend, Jimmy Lovinggood, Matt Crowley, Steve Danseglio, Peter Johnson, Rich Lichner, John Shephard, Steve Kehaya, Paul Buckley, Will Porteous

The Indicative Team and Fort Collins Team:

John Smith, Mark Smith, Angela Tucci, Jeff Millman, Tim Connor, Ron Bernal, Dave Dwyer, Wally Whitley, Christine Hudson, Glenn Price, Joe Broderick, Doug Johnson, Mike Freeman, Emily Kupec, Victor Holtorf, Allison Hines, Art Demaio, Chuck Hixson, Jill Shoemaker, Jimmy Lovinggood, Lindsay Roselle, Michelle Ware, Gloria Crockett, Terry Doonan, Steve Kehaya, Les Murphy

The JME, Neon, and Austin Team:

John Moores, Charlie Noell, Thilo Rochmann, Angela Tucci, Christine Hudson, Paul Viebrock, Craig Mullins, Jack Olson, Tom Harper, Kevin Sharp, Joe Farrell, Phil Sheridan, Preetish Nijhawan, Steve Kehaya, Paul Buckley, John Giglio, Eckhard Bogner, Abel Lomas, Andy Galewsky, Bryan Young, Chuck Hixson, Jim Hildner, Daniel Ramirez, Dave Haney and the Edwaney Clan, Dave Sunde, Norm Schoenfeld, Doug English, Kim Iverson, Leeann Roundtree, Tony Alagna, Roch DeSorbay, Roxanne Wilson, Tara Wood, Wayne Webb, Matt Farrell, Nate Hubbell

The Zehyr Team:

Keith Cook, Preetish Nijhawan, Samir Shah, Neeraj Gupta, Preethi Balasubramanian, Deepa Esturi, Roopa Sharma, Francis Adanza, Bill Mock, Eric McVey, John Torres, Karthik Selvakumar, Sanjay Zalavadia, Shailesh Mangal, Kyle Rosier, Mehron Latifi, Ray Watts, Teresa Baglietto, Chris Verna

The Providence Solutions Team:

Ricky Caplin, Juan Diaz, Nikki Featheringill, Matthew Kaiser, Les Murphy, Jeremiah Krumpf, Tiffanie Hughes, Matt Fenner, George Rich, Ken Purcell, Glenn Price, Teresa Baglietto, Sukhrob Karimov, Greg Jones, Lee Shipman, Tom Nolan, Teri Watkins, TJ Kent, JB Cross, Don Coleman

My Friends and Colleagues:

Thomas Charlton, Bob Ortalda, Chris Pepin, Han Bruggeling, Henry Charlton, Mr Bob Charlton, Paul Throdahl, Jerry Murdoch, Jeff Horing, Jim Bracher, Jeff Bixler, John Merritt, Kevin Comerford, Marc Valani, Kitty Puzon, Mike Yakura, Mike White, Ed Schoenbart, Rick Teed, Rob DePinto, Vinny Smith, John Andrews, Sudipto Banerjee, Tammie Faber, Kim Newton, Ali Ahmad-Pai, James Dalessandro, Marc Vogel, Shanda Bahles

And the Direct Contributors:

To my good friend and collaborator whose memory of so many great times was far better than mine, Phil Sheridan. I can't thank you enough. Without your help this book would never have gotten finished.

To my daughters, D'Anne, Jennifer, Sara, and Juli and my stepsons Sulton and Mehron; you were the inspiration and motivation behind the experiences that have shaped not just my career and this book but my entire life. Thank you!

LEADERSHIP

1. Power and authority can be used up. Leadership is a privilege. Treat it that way.

The fastest way to lose your authority or control is to overuse or abuse it. Power is something you use up. Every time anyone with power exercises it over others, they have less of it left afterward.

People will only stand for so much of someone exercising control over them. Use your power and authority cautiously and rarely. People always have the option of walking out the door.

However, a byproduct of power and authority is influence, and that you do not use up. It is sustainable and renewable and, if used fairly and with consideration, it even increases when you use it. Others are not intimidated or annoyed by the use of influence as they can be by the use of authority.

If you are fortunate enough to be in a position of authority, never forget your true responsibility is to serve those you lead and continue to earn the right to lead them every day. Do that wisely and fairly, and you will never need to look back over your shoulder. Those you are leading will always be there.

2. It's important to know what you're good at. Even more is important to know what you're not good at.

In a scene from the movie Magnum Force, Clint Eastwood's character Harry Callahan, a San Francisco cop, has confronted Lieutenant Briggs, the leader of a group of vigilante cops. The scene does not end well for Lieutenant Briggs. As Harry watches Lieutenant Briggs drive away, his car explodes with a bomb Harry had discretely activated. Then Harry says to himself "A man's gotta know his limitations."

It's satisfying to tackle a problem or take on a challenge that's in your wheelhouse when it's something you know you can do well. But taking on a challenge that you don't do well can make you miserable and may even put your job at risk. That's not to say you shouldn't always be looking for opportunities that challenge you and allow you to grow. Of course you should. But everyone should know beforehand their chances for success based on a keen analysis of their own capabilities.

Of course, you may not know if you're good at something until you try it. But trying something new when the stakes are high may not be a good idea.

In a long and contentious lawsuit in which my company was engaged with a Fortune-50 adversary, I was being deposed. The opposing attorney conducting the deposition kept having me read extensive excerpts from one of the legal documents at issue. After each reading, he kept trying to get me to tell him what it meant. Eventually, out of frustration, I replied to one of his, "Mr. Edwards, can you tell me what you just reads means?" I exploded with, "Counselor, if your goal is to prove that I know how to read, then I think you have accomplished that. But interpreting legal documents is not what I am qualified to do. From this point on, let me save you some time. My reply to every question regarding what this document means will be "I cannot answer that because interpreting legal documents is not something I am qualified to do."

Although I was tempted to try to respond to his line of questioning, not far into the deposition I realized that I was out of my depth. Had I continued to try and do so, I would have certainly done more harm than good.

3. Never overreact. Handle whatever comes with calm, cool confidence.

One of the most talented CEOs I've had the pleasure of working with is Thomas Charlton. I've mentored Thomas for more than twenty years and gave him his first CEO opportunity when I was executive chairman of Tidal Software. Two of Thomas's greatest strengths are his passion and intensity, but early on I had to counsel him to control and manage those strengths.

As Tidal was nearing the end of a critical quarter, an important deal was nearing conclusion. The sales rep managing the deal had left the office and locked his office door and file cabinets containing critical documents needed to close the deal. The rep was nowhere to be found, nor was he responding to phone calls. Needless to say, Thomas was furious.

Thomas took a hammer and crowbar, ripped the door off its hinges and pried open the file cabinet while the office staff stood and watched. He got what he needed and did close the deal, but the fear and discomfort he created with the office staff who were watching was unhealthy to say the least. Although I was happy Thomas closed the deal, I had the first of many conversations along these lines with this enormously talented young leader.

That conversation began with, "Thomas, you've got to manage your frustration, control your anger, and learn to accomplish what you need to accomplish without scaring the hell out of everyone around you."

Although it took a while, Thomas has come a long way. It's been years since I've heard words like hammer and crowbar used to describe how Thomas solved a problem.

A leader's responsibilities is to maintain a level head and help others do the same. Nothing good comes when fear, panic, confusion, and chaos rule. Our job as leaders is to show our team how to handle themselves in situations that are headed south fast. Seeing their leader overreact gives them permission to do the same. Don't grant them that permission.

4. As a leader, you never have to raise your voice.

As a leader who carries career and livelihood control over others, you should never raise you voice to anyone. As a matter of fact, you never need to raise your voice, not to mention that it's unprofessional, rude, and unbecoming of someone in a position of authority. There are far more effective ways of demonstrating you are unhappy.

In a situation where you may be tempted to raise your voice and you need to get someone's attention, whispering can be far more effective. If a situation is out of control and the person behind the problem needs to know what they are doing or have done is seriously not acceptable, just look at them silently and say nothing. They will get the message.

This is a lesson I learned from one of my negative mentors. I once reported to a vice president (VP) and general manager (GM) of a division of the company I was working for. He was one of those types who yelled and screamed at almost everyone. He fit the definition of a tyrant perfectly. Very few people survived reporting directly to him for very long. Most quit, and those who tried to stay often ended up getting fired during one of his tantrums. Although he never launched one of his tirades at me, I watched him destroy a number of capable and talented people. But seeing how wrong he was to treat people this way was a valuable learning experience for those of us who saw it. Watching how damaging he was when he did so, I promised myself I would never raise my voice to anyone in my professional life.

Ironically, he was eventually fired by someone who was more of a tyrant than he was. He got very little sympathy from anyone when that happened.

5. Don't be afraid to change your mind.

As a leader, it's important to be decisive and consistent. People need to know you've thought your decisions through and are willing stand behind what you say you are going to do.

But if new information, not previously known, comes to light or you see you've misjudged something, reversing course may be the wise choice. Just don't make a habit of it.

6. Self-awareness is the skill that prevents you from being a total jackass.

We've all met these types. The self-absorbed egomaniac who begins most sentences with "I." Those who, upon hearing that someone got their arm cut off, reply "Oh, that reminds me, I got a new watch." Those who lack the ability to be self-aware will not likely succeed in leadership roles.

The opposite of being self-aware is narcissistic. Unfortunately, I'm not sure self-awareness is something that is teachable. But if you even suspect you don't have enough of it, do the world a favor and get counseling.

7. Effective communication skills are vital to your success.

There are few skills that can contribute more to your success than your ability to skillfully and effectively communicate with others. Being able to express your thoughts and ideas is vital. Being able to do so with a minimal number of words, being clear and concise, is not just vital it is also exceptional and rare. We've all had to painfully listen while someone rambles on, talking way too much and repeating themselves, so much so that we can even forget what they're talking about. It is doubtful if those who do that realize they are doing it. I've often noticed that the more someone knows about a subject, the fewer words it takes for them to explain it.

Learning and developing the skill to deliver your thoughts and ideas clearly and concisely is a most worthwhile effort.

8. To be a great communicator, you must be a great listener.

It is rumored that Steve Jobs, during his second tenure as Apple CEO, carried a business card with the title Head Listener.

Being a good listener is a skill that can be learned. Following are a few simple techniques that can get you started:

- Ask questions
- Listen carefully to the answer, always letting the other person finish talking

- Repeat back what you hear, summarizing when appropriate
- Do not interrupt
- Maintain eye contact
- Don't allow yourself to be distracted (i.e., turn off your phone)
- Ask questions to ensure understanding
- Listen for meaning beyond the words (tone and body language)
- Be attentive and thoughtful
- Don't finish listening before the other person has finished talking

9. Well-developed and polished public speaking skills will take you a long way.

Few things you will ever do can make a bigger difference in your career faster than the ability to deliver an interesting, relevant, and powerful speech. Highly developed public speaking skills can get you promoted, elevate your peer group standing, get you elected to public office, change the way others look at you, establish you as a leader, engender admiration and respect from others, and separate you from the crowd more effectively than anything I know.

I had a peer early in my career where we were both regional VPs. He was a really nice guy and everyone liked him, but his leadership skills were almost non-existent. I watched him personally take credit for the accomplishments of his team and consistently hide when tough decisions needed to be made. Few of the managers who reported to him respected him.

His public speaking skills, however, were legendary. He could captivate a crowd better than anyone I had ever seen. He was asked to speak at every company meeting. His ability to inspire and motivate from the podium held everyone in awe, so much so that he was continually promoted and given leadership roles and responsibilities far beyond his abilities. He often left disastrous organizational issues in his wake, only to be given more advancement and promotions.

My point again is that great public speaking skills can accelerate your career and gain you recognition and respect unlike anything else.

Although few people will ever have the skills and abilities to leave a crowd on the edge of their seats, almost anyone can develop public speaking skills that will get you noticed and separate you from the masses.

We have all heard that the number-one fear humans have is public speaking. If that is true, and if you are willing to work on it, doing so can give you a great advantage because very few people will be willing to take the time and effort to become better public speakers.

Here are some guidelines for developing good public speaking skills:

- Talk about something you know well.

- Do your research and allow plenty of time for preparation.

- Tell stories about your experiences and the experiences of others.

- Know exactly what you are going to say before you stand up.

- Don't try to say too much. Make no more than two or three main points.

- Be cautious using humor until you are comfortable in front of a crowd.

- Practice giving your complete speech aloud at least twenty-five times (I'm serious about that number).

- If you have the opportunity to give the same speech to multiple audiences, do so.

  The more you do it, the better you will be at it. And you will love the feeling of accomplishment and the attention you get after delivering a good speech.

10. Never stop building your personal resume. Stay interesting and relevant.

Having interesting hobbies and the abilities to do things most people can't sets you apart and makes you more interesting. Always look for ways to add to your skill sets and abilities. Learn to fly an airplane, sail a boat, drive a racecar, play a musical instrument, become a rock climber, a hot-air balloon pilot…

In 2005, I moved to Fort Collins, Colorado, to take over as CEO of Indicative Software. Indicative was a spinoff from

HP/Agilent. Coming from Silicon Valley, it was common when first meeting someone to ask "What do you do?" The response was almost always about that kind of work they do, that is, "I'm an engineer, I work for Google or Oracle or Apple, and so on." In Colorado, I found that same question would often be answered with what they spend their time doing when they are not working, that is, "I'm a fly fisherman, I'm a rock climber, I'm a mountain biker … ." Immediately I found those people to be more interesting, and it made me want to get to know them.

Having the ability to do interesting things will immediately set you apart, make you more memorable and more interesting, and garner more respect, especially when they are skills that are challenging to master.

11. Always have a couple of well-rehearsed entertaining stories ready to tell.

The ability to instantly step up to the microphone and spontaneously entertain a crowd for a few minutes is extremely rare. It can make you the envy of everyone present. The trick is for it to appear spontaneous when actually you are both well prepared and well rehearsed. I'm not referring to the ability to stand up and tell the audience who you are and what you do. I mean delivering a polished, entertaining, crowd-pleasing short speech.

Invest the time to memorize two or three entertaining—either funny or moving stories—and rehearse them frequently enough so you are always prepared to deliver them without notice. It's one of those things that will make you memorable and will seriously impress people.

I served as executive in residence for the Rocky Mountain Innosphere, a powerful incubator and accelerator for several successful companies, and was attending an event for entrepreneurs in Fort Collins, Colorado, when I was unexpectedly asked to speak to the group for a few minutes. I stood up and spontaneously delivered one of my memorized stories. Sitting in the room was the president of the local Chamber of Commerce. After my five-minute talk, he approached me and asked if I would be the keynote speaker for their upcoming annual awards event for local businesses. I, of course, said yes. There were a few hundred people attending the awards event. My visibility in the business community skyrocketed, and I quadrupled my Colorado rolodex.

12. Do not over explain.

If anyone has ever told you that you talk too much, pay attention. We all know how annoying it is to listen to someone who rambles on when everyone long ago figured out what they were saying. Breaking that habit is difficult if not impossible, but anyone who does that should, at a minimum, develop strategies to try and control it.

I once had an executive in one of my companies who was unable to net it out. His descriptions of situations or answers to questions always took at least three times as long as needed. I started to avoid inviting him to meetings or having him participate in important discussions with others present because his propensity to ramble on either severely limited, or eliminated altogether, the willingness of others to participate. Unfortunately for him and the company, although he was smart and insightful and often looked at a situation with a unique perspective others missed, we were unable to fully take advantage of that skill. Most of the time, people stopped listening long before he got to his point.

I tried to coach him, but never made much progress. I eventually learned to accept his rambling and leverage his unique perspectives, but no one else he worked with could. I thought about bringing him with me to my next opportunity, but when I suggested it to my team I got a unanimous "Hell, no!" in response.

If you know that you are one of those people who talks too much and over explains, work on it. Seek help. Unless you address this problem, you will be forever limited.

13. Being comfortable should frighten you.

In many life pursuits, the goal is finding a comfortable position that relieves stress levels and where you find contentment. But when it comes to building and growing a business, being comfortable can never be your goal. When the final day of each quarter ends, it means that tomorrow morning you will be behind.

Many times in my career I've been told I need to learn to stop and celebrate achievement or success, but that has never been something I think of unless someone reminds me. There are many others who are the same way. But even when I'm reminded, I have a hard time doing it.

One of the keys to success is a fast start, and getting ahead out of the gate gives you a big advantage. Playing catch-up because you had a slow start is very difficult to overcome. Because of those two facts, I decided a long time ago that there may come a time to seek a comfortable position, but that time has not yet come.

Being comfortable today would still scare me.

14. Persistence will almost always win.

Early in my management career in the 1980s, I was the San Francisco branch manager for Informtics Software. We had been competing for a large opportunity worth several hundred thousand dollars a month at a local financial firm. One afternoon, my sales team came back to the office from an appointment at the financial firm looking really down. They had just been told that the decision was made to stay with their current vendor and they would not be moving forward with us.

I knew we were offering a better solution, and got angry when I heard the news. I pulled my team together and we spent well into the night developing an aggressive, all-points strategy to turn the decision around. It involved attacking at every angle and chasing down every person in the decision matrix, trying to overwhelm them. It was risky and we knew we could offend some of them, but we did it anyway. We had nothing to lose.

After about two weeks of our aggressive, persistent sales strategy, I got a call from the CFO informing me they had reversed their decision and were ready to sign our contract. He later told me that our persistence and determination compared with our competitor's low-key response was the reason they changed their mind.

The reason persistence, determination, and drive will win so often is that most people don't have persistence, determination, and drive.

15. Only fight the battles where the effort is worth the win.

When my oldest daughter, D'Anne, was in high school she was a complete social butterfly, so she seldom found time to clean her room. I, on the other hand, probably had never in my life left home before making my bed and hanging up my clothes. To say we had a few conflicts over that would be an understatement. That was until I realized this was a battle I was never going to win, and the price I was paying by just trying was too high.

I remember the day I finally said to myself, *I cannot let this issue dominate my relationship with my daughter.* So D'Anne and I came to a simple agreement. She kept the door to her room closed and I stopped bringing up the topic of whether or not her room was clean. I couldn't have been happier, and it made a huge difference to her that I was not always on her case.

Just because you have the right and authority to enforce rules or dictate behavior, it doesn't mean it is wise to do so.

Before taking on a challenge that will require others to give up something they would prefer not to, seriously consider the effort and if the outcome is worth the damage that enforcing your will on others may cause. Or better yet, find a simpler solution, like just closing the door.

16. Develop and exercise excellent questioning skills.

Knowing how to ask good questions is a powerful skill.

I'm a sailor and have chartered large power and sailboats in several places around the world. Most charter companies state in their application forms that before you will be allowed to take one of their expensive yachts for several days by yourself, you are required to take a sea trial—that is, go out on the water with the charter company so they can see that you know what you are doing. Before the sea trial, they do a walk around to familiarize you with the boat. After every walk around I've done, they have waived the sea-trial requirement. They did so because of the questions I asked. Only with knowledge and experience will you know the right questions to ask.

Back in the 1970s, Xerox turned their sales training into a product and delivered it to other companies. Attendees at the Xerox Sales Training all wore big buttons on their shirts or coats that simply said "Oh!" Part of the training was for them to ask someone a question, and no matter what the answer was they would reply "Oh!" That response caused the other to person continue talking and explain their answer in more detail. It really works. Try it on the next person you see.

Useful techniques for effective questioning and/or interrogation include:

- Ask questions that begin with how and why.
- Allow a pause after they stop speaking.
- Maintain direct eye contact.
- Show no emotion.
- Do not nod in agreement, just hold a steady gaze.
- Do not fold your arms while they are speaking.
- If they make a bold statement, raise your eyebrows and reply, "Oh, really?"

Use the above questioning techniques cautiously, as they can intimidate or make many people uncomfortable. I also suggest not using these techniques with your significant other.

Good questioning skills carry an obvious benefit. In any situation, a big advantage goes to the person with the most information.

17. Insecurity is the Achilles Heel of a leader.

An insecure leader can do more damage than you can imagine in a very short time. This often comes in the form of either indecisiveness or overbearing execution of simple decisions. Insecure leaders are often more consumed with how they look to others than with obtaining results. Not listening, not asking the right questions, and not being open to feedback are a few of the danger signals.

As a leader, you must be open to being challenged, albeit respectfully so. No one is right all of the time. But an insecure leader typically will not handle not being right well. Leaving such a person in that role is not only unfair to their direct reports it's unfair to the leader as well, since it is unlikely they will succeed. It's far better to move them to an individual contributor role if that's possible. But leaving them in a leadership role is a mistake. Trying to solve this problem will take more time than you probably have and is unlikely to succeed anyway.

18. When it comes to recruiting and hiring the right people, some are very good at it, others not so much.

Your ability to identify and recruit high-caliber talent that fits well into your organization will either be a great asset and one of the reasons you succeed or, if you don't have that ability, will be one of the reasons you struggle.

Many technology companies are founded by brilliant engineers with underdeveloped people-judgment skills. Thus, they end up with a cast of ill-fitting staff members with little ability to accomplish the difficult task of building a company together.

I served as a board member for a founder steeped in the technology, and he knew his products better than anyone. All of the skills he used in designing and developing software he tried to use to evaluate the people he recruited, which was to say that he analytically evaluated their skills and the experience stated on their resume with what he thought he needed for the job. He was looking for an exact match in their background to fit what he perceived as the requirements of the job.

That process when you are hiring engineers may work sometimes, but when it comes to hiring sales, marketing, and leadership talent, that same process can cause you to miss out on some very good people. I watched him reject some amazingly talented sales and marketing candidates with remarkable track records because they had not sold to the same customers the same type of products his company had built. I could not convince him that learning a new product and figuring out how to sell to a new type of customer was a very manageable transition, and having excellent sales skills and a strong work ethic were more important.

Along with his over-analytic skills approach, he also had no ability to judge candidates on cultural fit, work ethic, and the many other intangibles that go into making someone right for the job, the team, and the company.

Some people, though, have an additional sense when it comes to evaluating people. There are times when they just know when the candidate is exactly what they are looking for.

In the late 1980's when we were building XA Systems and I was still the VP of sales, I was staffing the Chicago sales office. A candidate I was interviewing named John Figliulio didn't have all of the right experience on his resume, but fifteen minutes into the interview I knew he was what I was looking for. John had an energy and charisma about him that could light up the room. I hired John, and he went on to become one of the most successful salesmen in XA's history. After XA, John's career continued to excel and he became a successful CEO. If I had only tried to match the experience on his resume with the job requirements, I would not have hired him and I would have missed out on one of the best team members I ever worked with.

Another key factor in identifying talent is to look at how pure are their motives. A story I still tell today about John is during the interview when I asked him what had been his largest earnings year to date in his career. He replied, "Lacy, I'm actually not that motivated by money." I replied, "John, that tells me you've never made much." A couple of years later, I presented John with one of the largest commission checks I've ever given anyone. The check had six figures. It was for one month's commission.

19. When you discover a super star...

If you are fortunate, there will be times in your career when you will work with individuals who have skills, talents, and an intellectual capacity that you realize are well beyond that of many others you have known.

If that happens, immediately begin devising plans so you can take that person with you wherever you go.

When I was being recruited to join Indicative Software in Fort Collins, Colorado, I interviewed and was interviewed by the Indicative executive team. One of them was VP of marketing, Angela Tucci. Little did I know at the time that I was sitting across from one of the smartest people I'd ever meet.

Angela's education credentials were impressive, a degree in physics from Princeton University and a Stanford MBA, but I've met several highly educated yet ineffective people. That was not the case with her.

For the next seven years, first at Indicative then as my chief strategy officer at JME, the private equity firm owned by John Moores, I observed numerous times Angela's insight and ability to see past the noise and lay bare the facts that others overlooked. Her analytic skills combined with amazing intellectual capacity were unparalleled.

All of this combined with top-notch people skills, drive, determination, unmatched work ethic, and discipline put Angela in a category by herself.

The reason I'm writing about Angela is to say that if you ever cross paths with someone of a caliber far above others you encounter, latch on to them, treat them well, and keep them with you for as long as you can. Over those years, I gave Angela many of my most-challenging problems and not once was I disappointed with the results.

Not surprisingly, today Angela is a successful CEO and I am proud of her success. If I had a hand in helping her along the way, I was honored to do so.

20. Your answer to most requests should probably be no the first time they ask. Make them justify it.

No is a powerful word, while yes is easy to regret. Statements like "I'm not convinced" or questions like "What is your plan B if we don't do this?" can start meaningful discussions that often result in a better choice. And it is always better to have someone defend their ideas and suggestions. They will inherently get better because of it. You also find out what is really important. An interesting scenario I've observed many, many times is when I've rejected a proposal and then asked about it a few days later, I was then told, "I decided we didn't need that anyway." It has always amazed me how so many people, given a little time, will talk themselves out of doing something they insisted was vital just a short time ago.

21. When someone brings you a problem, your first question should always be "So what do you propose to do about it?"

If the response to your question is they don't know what to do, suggest they go think about it and come back with a couple of suggestions. Most often, however, they will already have a proposal or recommendation.

Like most decisions, addressing problems needs to be handled by the person with the most information about the situation and the most at stake.

Your team members may want you to solve their problems for them. Don't be so quick to do that. Your role should be to determine who needs to own the problem and help them find the solution.

22. Creating pressure is part of a leader's job. Just be sure it's positive pressure, not negative pressure.

Applying pressure in a constructive way can cause everyone's performance to go up, no matter what your job. That's true for CEOs as well as assembly-line workers. We all respond to positive pressure to try harder, work harder, and produce better results.

The problem is when negative pressure is applied, the kind that leaves you feeling threatened or unappreciated. We've all had it, felt it, and probably have been guilty of doing it ourselves.

Being aware of how you are coming across to others can make a difference in whether the results are motivational and inspire your team to want to work harder or leave them resentful, with no desire to contribute more.

23. Build your go-to team and treat them well so you can take them with you.

Over the years, I've been very fortunate to have hired several talented, hardworking, dedicated, and loyal team members. It is those people who deserve the credit for any success I have enjoyed in my career. My role, primarily, was to support them, treat them fairly, recognize their contributions, pay them well, and, most importantly, let them do the job I hired them to do.

As I moved from opportunity to opportunity, and whenever I had a position open that was right for one of my former team members, I sought them out and invited them to join me. Consequently, there is a long list of former team members that I have worked with five or six times over the past thirty years.

When I took over as executive chairman of John Moores Equity, the CEO of one of the companies, Neon Enterprise Software, resigned, so I decided to take over the company myself rather than recruit a new CEO. About a year into the engagement, we launched a new product that required an entirely new worldwide sales team, sales management, sales-support teams, and new engineering management. We had immediate open positions for twenty-one team members. In a period of a little more than ninety days, I recruited and filled all twenty-one positions with people I had worked with before, except a single position.

If I had gone to the open market to recruit and hire that team, the headhunter fees alone would have been more than $500,000, not to mention it would have taken at least a year to find and hire them. By going to people I knew, every member of the team was proven, committed, and ready to go on day one.

24. When hiring for critical roles, know exactly what you're looking for and do not compromise.

When I was hired as president of Unison Software, I knew I would have to re-build the world-wide sales teams. I needed to move from a predominantly inside-sales approach to a direct-enterprise sales model, and the first role that needed to be filled was vice president of sales.

The company had not been focusing on enterprise accounts, so I had to have someone who knew how to get into, how to sell, and how to close opportunities in the multi-hundred-thousand-dollar range, as well as someone with direct knowledge of our market, which was enterprise job scheduling. The average deal size previously had been around $20,000. I made a list of the experience and all of the skills the person must have and reviewed it in detail with the recruiters. I started interviewing in September, and over the next four months I interviewed twenty-seven different people. Many were good candidates, some of whom I had worked with before, but until number twenty-seven walked in, I was never completely satisfied.

Candidate number twenty-seven was John Ferraro. John came from Computer Associates, where he was a regional sales manager. One characteristic John had that I liked was an intense hunger for material success. He had seen several peers reach significant levels of wealth, and he badly wanted that for himself. John came from selling a competitive product in the exact marketplace we were in and had a notably successful track record.

I could have easily selected one of the other candidates, but none of them checked all of the boxes the way John did, and the success he produced at Unison was historic. Our average deal size went from $20,000 to more than $300,000 in his first year.

One of my favorite stories about John occurred a few quarters after we had gone public. We were entering the last day of the quarter and were still a few hundred thousand dollars short of our goal. I knew the damaging effect that failing to hit our quarterly revenue target would have on our stock price and company valuation. I was extremely nervous and couldn't sleep, so I got up at 4:00 a.m. and drove to the office. When I walked in at 5:00 a.m., John was already there on the phone with the CIO of Pillsbury yelling at him trying to get a deal closed. By the end of the day, we had hit our number.

Knowing exactly what I was looking for and not compromising on anything for this critical position was one of the key reasons we were able to turn Unison from a company about to be acquired for $14 million into a company worth close to $200 million in less than three years.

25. You are not doing anyone any favors leaving someone in a position where they are not succeeding.

When you terminate someone for performance reasons, you are being forced to make a career decision for them that they should be making for themselves.

Rarely have I terminated someone for performance reasons that it came as a surprise to them. They almost always knew they were not succeeding and were certainly not happy in the job.

I've had several former staff members contact me months after being terminated to thank me for pushing them to find a more fulfilling career.

26. It's okay to get pissed off. It's not ok to go crazy.

In one of my companies, I had a talented young engineer named Michael working on an important project for one of our largest customers. His technical skills were substantial, his work ethic was unquestionable, and his customer relations-management abilities were excellent. His business judgment, however, wasn't always on the mark. In the middle of the project, he made a judgment call that caused a setback so material we could have lost the account. I got directly involved and we were able to save the account, but it was close. I pulled the key staff members together afterward to go through what happened to prevent a recurrence. To say I was not happy would have been an understatement. At the end of the meeting, Michael stayed behind and asked to speak with me alone. His participation going forward was critical to the recovery and completion of the project. When we were alone he said, "I know you're upset and I assume you want my resignation." I looked back at him and said, "Michael, yeah, I'm pissed-off, but I'm not crazy! We have no chance of recovering without your participation. Now get your chin up and get back to work!"

You may have heard the story about an employee who made a mistake that cost his company $1 million. After it was discovered, the man went to his manager and said, "I guess you are going to fire me." His manager looked at him and said, "Fire you? I just spent $1 million on your education! Why would I fire you now?"

27. Reject ideas and proposals with humor. You want them to keep coming back with more.

I once had a talented and aggressive marketing VP for Europe, Middle East, Africa (EMEA) named Chris working in our London office who was consistently pushing the envelope. He got a lot of good things done, but if left up to him he would overspend on questionable projects. Chris would often come to me and pitch programs, events, and activities that were not well thought out. Once, after a long and detailed presentation on an expensive marketing campaign that I was convinced was a bad idea, I told him so. But he continued to persist. After several attempts to convince me, I finally I looked at him and said, "Chris, remember those times when you were a kid and you were trying to convince your dad to let you do something and he kept saying no and you kept asking, 'But, Dad, why not?' He would eventually say, 'Because I am your dad and I say so, now don't ask again!' Well Chris, this is one of those times!"

28. As the leader, don't let them know what you're thinking too soon. Once you do, you may stop getting their ideas.

One of the most important roles a leader must play is soliciting thoughts and ideas from their staff. Getting their full contribution is vital. Collective intelligence is powerful, and some of the best ideas can come from quiet, low-key, intellectual types who may not readily speak up.

In my planning and strategy sessions, I try not to let anyone know what I am thinking and what my opinions are on what we are trying to figure out. I've found that once they know what I'm thinking, some of them will assume that is what we're going to do and the ideas stop coming.

It's best to get their thoughts, ideas, and suggestions out before you show your own thoughts. It's even better to get them to vote on directions and plans without you voting.

Your primary job is to lead the discussion, ask lots of questions, exhaust their flow of ideas, and be sure the best decisions get made.

29. Correct hiring mistakes quickly. When you think you have a problem, you almost always do.

In the early 1990s at XA Systems, I was looking for a VP of sales. I found a candidate and put him through a lengthy interview process. I had him meet with the entire executive management team and all of my board members. I even sent him to an outside consulting firm for a skills assessment and culture-fit analysis. Everything came back thumbs up. So, I hired him.

I had an off-site planning session scheduled before he could start work, but I asked him to attend the first day and a half of the planning session. We weren't four hours into the planning session before I knew I had made a serious mistake. After all of the interviews, profile analysis, and background checks, instead of digging in and understanding our organization, he felt he already knew what needed to be done and immediately started talking about changes he was going to make. I didn't hire him to come in and change the way we were doing business, I hired him to learn our way of doing things, lead the team, and keep it performing. We were already quite successful and weren't looking to make big changes.

Although I knew he wasn't going to work out, I left him in place for three months, partly because I was embarrassed that I had made such a big mistake and I knew it would reflect poorly on my judgment and decision making, and partly because he had resigned his current position to join us.

Even though I had solicited the opinions and input from all of the key stakeholders, I completely owned the decision to hire him. I tried to counsel and guide him, but his inability to change his approach led to his departure.

Although I stayed close to him and prevented any permanent damage, he did cause several disruptions and created lots of confusion. Looking back, I should have made the call and terminated him within the first thirty days and dealt with the fallout.

30. You will not truly know someone until you have worked with them for a while.

Interviews and background checks help, but in most situations when you've gotten to know someone well, there will be surprises. Hopefully they will be good surprises.

But few people are exactly what they appear to be when you first meet them. I'm not saying people are deceptive nor that they will intentionally mislead you, but it is wise over time to be open to your perceptions changing.

When you put a new hire in a critical role, be observant of their behavior and how they react to situations. You want to be sure the match you thought you had is close enough to what you need. It can often take six months or longer before you know for sure.

31. The farther the distance, the more important trust becomes.

When you are growing your business, expanding and opening new offices or additional locations is exciting. But the danger of losing control is high. People don't always follow directions or conform to your standards when they are many miles away and left on their own. Building a remote team with people you know you can trust is vital.

I once hired a branch manager in Los Angeles to open an office and hire a sales team. After a few of weeks, I started getting suspicious of his all-too-frequent unavailability. I started digging and doing some investigation and found out he never resigned his old job and was taking two paychecks. I called the CEO of the other company and we both fired him.

At XA Systems when we first opened direct European operations, I transferred Pat Neisen, one of my most trusted executives from the U.S. to relocate to Europe and set up and run the operation. Pat and I were in lock-step on what to do and how to do it. I knew that many U.S. software companies didn't get European sales operations functioning effectively until their second or third try. With this approach, we got it right the first time.

Since then, I have developed a strong network of trusted European team members, many whom I've worked with multiple times. One of them, Steve Kehaya, I've worked with in six different companies over the past thirty years. I've asked Steve to open up European operations and distribution networks a number of times, and have never had to worry about trust issues.

In some situations with remote operations, the risk can be more than financial.

At NEON Enterprise Software, I inherited a development center based in Eastern Europe. I realized fairly quickly that not everything was going the way it should, especially from a financial-management and reporting perspective. I tried to address the issues remotely, but could not make much progress. I then asked our president of European Operations, Thilo Rockmann to pay a visit and try and get control of the situation. After his first visit, Thilo and I reviewed what he learned and decided we needed to have a complete audit.

We hired an auditor and the audit was scheduled. Thilo scheduled another trip to meet with the auditors and to be onsite during the audit. On the night Thilo arrived, with the audit to begin the next day, the building that housed the entire development team and management for the operation burned to the ground.

Thilo was on the first flight out the next morning and we shut down the operation. Having people you can completely trust on your team is important. When you're doing business a half world away, complete trust is not just important, it is necessary.

32.   Be cautious when hiring exceptionally brilliant people, they must be closely managed. But sometimes it's not even possible.

I've been fortunate to work with some of the most talented engineers on the planet, the kind of people who can create algorithms and figure out how to make software do amazing things faster and more accurately than anyone thought possible. But some of them came with baggage and, in some cases, too much baggage.

I've had them destructively attack others who are not on their intellectual level, offend customers, try to quit in the middle of a project, and seriously disrupt the work of others, just to name a few of the challenges. People with ultra-high intelligence levels typically have a much lower frustration level because they see so much more than others. Unless you have a reporting and organizational structure to prevent opportunities for negative interaction, you will spend an inordinate amount of time picking up after them. In many cases, I've had such engineers report directly to me so I could better manage the fallout.

Another error that's easy to make is giving brilliant engineers leadership responsibilities. That is almost never a good idea unless you plan to spend a substantial amount of your time wearing a striped shirt with a whistle around your neck.

I had one such brilliant engineer on my team who had an IQ of at least 200. His engineering skills were scary. He built some algorithms for data analytics that only a small portion of the population could even comprehend. But the downside is that he offended almost everyone in the company. If he saw a marketing document, he re-wrote it and sent his version to the VP of marketing. He once sent one of his dissertations on a sales presentation he didn't agree with to the entire company. I spent a week talking my VP of sales and VP of marketing off the ledge. But he could not help himself.

My solution was to have him work from home and only communicate with me. This was long before the term tele-commuting had ever been used. If he needed to be in a meeting, I had to be present. I kept him on a short leash and had to frequently rein him in. It worked for the most part and we were able to leverage his remarkable talents, but it took a lot of my time.

33. Never put someone with an oversized ego is a position with significant responsibility. You will likely regret it.

One of the most important characteristics of a good leader is the ability to be self-aware. They must be able to look at themselves in the mirror and see at least a resemblance of what others see. They must be self-critical and be open to criticism. Those are things an oversized ego will not do, or at least not do well.

The really important decisions, those that have a significant effect on an organization, the more important it is to get them right the first time. That is a responsibility that must be in the hands of someone who solicits input, advice, and criticism, someone who will question themselves and will care more about the right decision being made than about them being right.

It's easy to spot an oversized ego, just ask them to tell you about the biggest mistake they've ever made. Their answer won't likely entail anything with serious consequences.

34. High morale when times are bad is impossible. Celebrating success is the only remedy.

During difficult times, companies will often try to manufacture improved morale through activities, incentive programs, celebrations, and so on. It does not work. Success is the only real morale booster. That's not to say high morale comes automatically with success. It doesn't. But attempts to improve morale when results are disappointing will not work. It's better to put that effort into improving results.

35. Your primary responsibility to your staff is to provide them with an opportunity to succeed.

Identify those who seize the opportunity given to them and leverage it to their and your advantage, then continue to support them and help them achieve. When you identify those who choose not to seize the opportunity, part company with them quickly to make room for someone who will.

36. Top performers versus dishonesty.

In one of my companies, as we were building our European sales teams, the sales executive I put in place recruited the top sales representative (rep) in the world from our direct competitor. He came in and quickly became our top sales rep. A couple of years later, my European sales executive called me and said, "I've got some really bad news. We're going to have to fire our best sales rep. He has been cheating on his expense reports." I learned that he had exaggerated entertainment expenses and mileage expenses. The total amount of the exaggeration was not significant, but it did happen. My response to my exec was, "Yes, this is disappointing, but you are not going to fire the top sales rep in the company over this." I told him to do the following: "In a non-threatening manner, show him the discrepancies, tell him in the future to be more accurate. Tell him no one else needs to know about this, then tell him how important he is and change the subject to a sales situation. Never let him know you told anyone, and especially never tell him you told me. However, watch him going forward and be cautious about giving him financial decision-making authority."

We all make mistakes and do things we regret, and most of us will make the most of second chances. In this situation, managing the downside was a far better solution than losing our top sales rep. He stayed with the company for many years and continued as a top performer.

Making the choice between dishonesty versus competence isn't as black and white as some would have you believe. Knowing I can depend on someone to get the job done but also knowing I need to double check the data I'm given may be a trade I'm willing to make. Everyone has a downside of some sort that we must manage and not allow it to destroy us. Some people sometime need a little help in managing theirs.

37. Constantly turn over the bottom 20 percent of performers.

Each year during annual performance reviews, I have my management teams rank their team members going from the most valuable to the least.

Measuring performance is one of the requirements of building and growing a business. As a leader, your job is to ensure all aspects of your company are performing well. If your team of high performers makes up 80 percent of your workforce, you have done an exceptional job of recruiting and hiring.

What that also means is 20 percent of your workforce needs performance improvement. Do not convince yourself that having 20 percent subpar performers is acceptable. You need to consistently work on improving the performance of everyone on your team and replacing those who are not measuring up. You're always going to have unplanned and unwanted turnover, even among your top performers. Use your improve-or-replace performance plans to backfill unplanned losses in your top performers.

38. There may be a time when, due to required confidentiality, you will have to lie.

In one of my companies, a competitor was trying to acquire us. The rumors had gotten out and the negative impact was significantly being felt. No one wanted to work for the competitor. We had successfully made them the enemy, recruited some of their top staff, and no one in our company had good things to say about them, especially their former staff members. But we were a venture-backed company, and if the financial terms were good enough the deal would no doubt go through. In the midst of these discussions, we had our annual sales kick-off meeting. In case the deal did not happen, I had to keep the sales team engaged and excited about the upcoming year. As was customary, I gave a speech to the worldwide sales team. At the end of my talk, someone raised their hand and asked me directly, "Are you still trying to sell the company to XYZ?" If I had been completely honest it could have been damaging to the company's future in case a deal didn't happen. I really needed everyone to get back to work doing what they could do to grow the company. Ironically, at that very moment, our lead investor was in the offices of the competitor trying to work out the details of a transaction. So I lied and said "No." I knew that anything other a complete denial would be interpreted as a yes.

About a week later, the acquisition was announced and the deal closed about ninety days after that. A number of people who were in the room when I said "No" later asked me why I lied. I answered that I was hired by our investors to protect their interests and sometimes to do that I am required to be less than forthcoming when put on the spot. They all understood, and I do not believe anyone thought less of me because of it.

39. When you have to fire someone, do it quickly.

The process I use when I have to terminate someone's employment is to call them into my office, stand and meet them at the door, close the door behind them, and, as I am walking to my chair, say to them, "Unfortunately, we are going to have to part company. Your employment is being terminated today."

I say that before I even sit down, only a few seconds into the meeting. I then say, "We can discuss as long as you wish the reasons for your termination, but the decision is final and there can be no discussion regarding changing it."

When you terminate someone's employment, you must have your facts straight and solid data to back up your decision. If you allow yourself to get drawn into a discussion on their specific activities, the person you are terminating knows far more about those than you do. It's much better to focus on performance and results and stay away from activities and day-to-day details.

One experience early in my management career taught me the need to be straightforward, specific, direct, and blunt. I had a sales rep who was not performing, and I made the decision that he just didn't have what it took to succeed in sales.

He was busy all the time, but doing nothing that would lead to closing a sale and was terrible at reading the interest level of a prospect. I called him into my office and said, "Rufus, I'm afraid your efforts are not going to pay off for you or us, so it's better for you to seek employment elsewhere." He said, "I've really been trying and I think things will turn around soon." I replied, "Unfortunately, I don't believe that so we need to wrap things up."

He left my office, and a few minutes later I told my assistant that Rufus had been terminated and asked her to make arrangements to get his keys and see if he needed help removing his personal items from the office. She came right back and asked, "Are you sure he knows he's been terminated?"

I went to his office and asked if he understood that I had terminated him. His reply was, "You meant now?"

40. You do not solve personnel problems by moving the personnel involved around.

Unless you've made a mistake by putting someone in a role not suited for their skill set, such as, taking one of your good pre-sales support reps and moving them into sales, moving people who are struggling from one position to another seldom solves the problem.

When you hire someone, you don't expect them to know all they need to know on day one. But the learning curve should be relatively short and you should see an accelerating increase in their growth. If they are still falling behind

and struggling after a few weeks, you should probably admit
your mistake and address it.

**41. When you promote someone to a position of increased
responsibility, look for an immediate surge in their growth and
performance. If you don't see it, you may have made a mistake.**

> New and added responsibility should come with excitement
> and a visible display of energy. You should see a quick surge
> in their development in the new role and be pleasantly sur-
> prised with their performance. When you see that, they are
> likely to succeed in the new position.

> When you don't see that excitement and surge, most of the
> time the promotion will turn out to have been a mistake.

**42. No matter how badly you feel when you have to terminate
someone's employment, never forget that it's much worse for
them.**

> If you've been in leadership long, you've undoubtedly had to
> have a termination discussion with one of your direct reports.
> And unless you have sociopathic tendencies, you felt awful
> and faced the occasion with feelings of dread. This is one of
> the down sides of leadership, and it does not get easier.

> Although, with experience, you get better at conducting the
> termination discussion and more skilled at handling the var-
> ious responses you get, you still have that feeling of, *I really
> wish I didn't have to do this* in your stomach.

Several years ago, I was counseling one of the members of my leadership team helping her prepare for a termination session with one of her team members and she was expressing how badly she felt about having to do the termination. Everyone liked that person, but they were not working out. I responded to her comment on how badly she felt with, "No matter how badly you feel, remember it's worse for them."

She came back to me a few days later and told me that she kept thinking about my comment and it really helped her to stop focusing on her own feelings and be more professional, compassionate, and considerate toward the person she terminated.

43. As a leader, value your team's uniqueness and talents in addition to their work.

A touching story as told by his son, Max, about DJ Depree, the founder of Herman Miller Furniture Company, in his book *Leadership Is an Art* published in 1987, illustrates this point.

In manufacturing plants, before mass electrical power distribution, the plants operated with steam engines. A small steam plant was located at the end of a long building and a shaft ran the length of the building. The steam engine turned the shaft, which had belts attached to it to turn the saws, lathes, and other equipment needed for the manufacturing plant.

The person responsible for keeping the steam engine running and the shaft turning for the belts was called the millwright. One day the millwright for Herman Miller died. It was the first time DJ Depree had an employee die, so he decided to go to the widow's home to express his condolences personally.

When he got to the home, after a few awkward minutes, the widow asked him if he would like to read some poetry. He said of course, and she handed him a leather bound book with numerous pages of beautiful poetry. After reading a few pages, he asked the widow who the poet was. She replied that her husband, the millwright, was the poet.

Still today at Herman Miller, after many years, the question is often asked "Was the employee who died a millwright who wrote poetry or was he a poet who did millwright work?"

STARTING, BUILDING, AND GROWING A BUSINESS

44. What it takes to launch a company:

- Identified Market opportunity
- Products(s) or services that effectively address the market opportunity
- Execution

I have attended and/or participated in numerous venture-capital (VC) conferences that bring together entrepreneurs and investors. The top *Takeaway* from those experiences is that the smart money always follows market opportunities over interesting products or smart people. I have also attended a number of angel-investor conferences and observed that many of the angel investors end up following interesting products and charismatic entrepreneurs. The majority of the VC firms I know make money. Very few angel investors that I know do.

At XA Systems, we were raising a Series C round of funding in 1990 and were presenting to Sequoia Capital, the legendary Sand Hill Road VC firm. As part of Sequoia's process,

I was asked to present to all of Sequoia's partners. A few of my slides included bios of my management team. I probably went on a little too long on that topic, and finally Don Valentine, one of the founding partners at Sequoia interrupted me and said, "Lacy, I don't need to hear any more about your management team. If you're not good enough we'll throw you out anyway. What I'm interested in is your market opportunity." My *Takeaway* … "Message received!"

Once you have identified a growing and well-defined market opportunity, a competitive product to effectively address the opportunity is next. To effectively address means customers will want to buy your product and pay you enough for it so you can make money with it. I've seen numerous software products that are over engineered, too costly to build, and too hard to use. They may have been good ideas, but they never achieved any material success because they missed too many of the key points required to succeed.

The simplified definition of successful execution is selling enough of your product fast enough. Looking back at the phrase time is money, the longer it takes to sell your product the lower your probability of success. Long sales cycles are expensive. Many times, they are too expensive.

Obviously there are numerous components of successful execution, but you must be in a thriving, growing market with a good product that people need and are willing to pay enough for it quickly enough. If you're not, then none of the rest of it matters.

45. Above all else, place your stakeholders' interests first.

Above staff members and customers, your decisions must place stakeholder interest first in all situations. By stakeholders, I am referring to owners, shareholders, and investors.

Your first reaction to hearing this may be, *Unless you take care of customers and staff members, stakeholders could lose everything*. That, of course is correct, but therein is your answer. Placing stakeholder interest first means never making a decision on behalf of customers or staff members that does not have positive impact on stakeholders. Put another way, never make a decision on behalf of a customer or staff member that is not also in the best interest of your stakeholders.

A CEO's single most important responsibility is to increase stakeholder value. If you find yourself being tempted to place your stakeholders' interests second, you are on your way out. Stakeholders decide whether you should stay or go. If they ever see that you are not placing their interests first, you will be replaced.

46. Your worst enemy is time.

Striving for success at anything comes with a time clock attached. No matter what you're trying to accomplish, your biggest risk will almost always be running out of time.

One of the biggest challenges of being an entrepreneur is overcoming optimism. But optimism is a required ingredient for being an entrepreneur. Where optimism usually gets you in trouble is expecting results sooner than is realistic. Nothing happens when you think it will, and everything takes longer than expected. If you are building a business plan to do something you've never done before, be sure to include a significant fudge factor, especially when it comes to elements in your plan that require considerable use of cash.

Your plan needs to be written, detailed, well thought out, and must include the most important component of any business plan, a cash-flow forecast.

It's not ironic that companies run out of time and money at the exact same point.

47. Develop and refine your elevator pitch to perfection.

Although the amount of time you will spend getting your elevator pitch perfect will be excruciatingly long and even brain numbing at times, spend whatever time it takes to perfect it.

Your goal should be to be to clearly and concisely tell someone who does not know your business what you do, how you do it, and why it's important during a twenty-second elevator ride.

Then make everyone in the company memorize it and be able to recite it. You will have to test them frequently, or most won't have it committed to memory.

48. Build the easiest-to-buy and easiest-to-use products in the business.

Our first venture capital investment in XA Systems came from TVI (Technology Venture Investors), the legendary Sand Hill Road VC firm that was the sole venture investor in Microsoft. Dave Marquardt, the cofounder of TVI, served on the Microsoft board of directors from 1981 to 2014.

The partner at TVI who made the investment in XA was Bob Kagle. XA was one of Bob's first deals at TVI. After TVI declared victory and closed out its fund in 1995, Bob cofounded Benchmark Capital, whose investment successes include eBay, Uber, Twitter, Snapchat, Instagram, and Yelp, just to name a few.

Bob served on our board at XA Systems from 1985 until XA was acquired by Compuware in 1991. During those years, I learned many things from him, but one lesson was a phrase Bob used during one of our board meetings when we were discussing our new product-development strategy. Bob said, "What you need to do is build the easiest-to-use and easiest-to-buy software products in the business." So simple, yet so profound. I've carried that lesson with me and have used it in every company since.

49. Not many companies fail because they are too focused.

Many, however, fail because they are not focused enough. There is a reason KFC has never sold hamburgers.

This comes down to what you want to be known for. As an early-stage company, you must identify yourself with something people will remember. Whatever it is you decide on, focus on being the best at it and stick to it, backing it up with good products and legendary customer service.

50. Raising investment capital is hard and getting harder.

Probably the most difficult effort any entrepreneur can undertake is raising investment capital. Even getting an appointment to pitch your opportunity is more challenging than what many are up to.

If you're going down the VC route, knowing the VC firm's investment profile upfront can be useful. Being able to target specific market interest may help. But the biggest challenge is still going to be getting someone's attention.

During hot markets, the sheer number of opportunities VC firms are flooded with is staggering. Breaking through the noise and getting noticed can be extremely difficult. A personal introduction can make all the difference, but they can also be hard to come by. I get several calls each year from entrepreneurs asking for introductions to my contacts in the investment community. I rarely comply. Unless it's someone I know well and have insights into their business, I decline.

Also, gone are the days of getting attention from investors for a concept or idea. Today, without a functional product and, in some cases, paying customers, raising money from a VC firm will be difficult.

So what about angel investors? The investment criteria for angel investors is quite different from VC firms. Access to angel investors is not as difficult. Many angel investor networks exist and are open to inviting entrepreneurs in to pitch their opportunities.

Having spent substantial amounts of time with both VC firms and angel investors, I've noticed a few significant differences. VCs investments are driven by market opportunities, while angel investors can be heavily swayed by the personality, passion, and charisma of the entrepreneur.

Another difference is the amount of due diligence by each. VC firms do many times the due diligence of angels. Most have full-time analysts and researchers. Angels typically rely on their personal networks. Data on results suggest VC firms will have a significantly positive return on two in ten investments while angel investors range from one in ten to one in twenty, and seldom are the returns significant.

The best way may be to bootstrap it until you have a real product and a handful of paying customers. By then, you may be able to get the interest of investors. Another approach could be a partnership with a company who already has sales and marketing with current customers who can buy your product. That route can produce a much shorter path to success.

The other possibility is money from friends and family. My advice on this has always been: Don't do it. Your mother thinks you are smarter than Bill Gates. You're probably not. If you can't convince sophisticated investors to invest in your company, they are sending you an important message. Don't ignore it.

51. What you really get with a Venture Capital investment.

When a VC firm invests in your company, by far their most valuable contribution is money. VC firms hire some of the most intelligent people around. Unfortunately, being highly intelligent can sometimes come with downsides, like having a high degree of impatience and suffering from the smartest-guy-in-the-room syndrome. That combination has caused the decline and subsequent failure of several promising startups.

In the early 2000s, I was sought out as a consultant and advisor by a document-management software company that had been reduced to two engineers/founders. They had a handful of customers paying just enough for the two of them to live comfortably. When they brought me in, the document-management market was exploding and they needed a couple of million dollars to invest in their product to effectively compete and to hire a couple of sales reps.

Two years earlier, they had raised $10 million from three well-known VC firms. The VC-loaded board hired a high-priced VP of sales from Oracle, several expensive sales reps, and an overloaded marketing team.

Not surprisingly, with a big-company background sales team that did not fully comprehend the challenges of a startup, they burned through all of the investment in less than eighteen months and produced no meaningful sales revenue.

Due to the disappointing sales results, none of the VC firms were interested in participating in another round, they all resigned from the board, and the company slipped into the living-dead category.

Worth noting, of the VC-stacked board, none of them had more than three years of experience except one individual. When I met with that one experienced investor to understand what happened, I found him to be one of the most rude, arrogant jerks I've ever met. Since that meeting, I've spoken with several people who know him and everyone describes him the same way.

In this situation, the VC money was a plus, but almost everything else was a minus. Unfortunately, the minuses were too many and wiped out the money.

This scenario reminds me of a phrase several people used during those days: That many in the VC community were high on OPM (Other People's Money).

52. Some VC firms have a reputation for being poor on follow through and not fulfilling commitments.

But that is not always true. Some I've worked with are amazingly effective and have made a big difference.

An example of one of the best VC firms around is RRE Ventures, LLC, founded by James D. Robinson III, the former chairman and CEO of American Express, his son James D. Robinson IV, and Stuart Ellman.

Having spent seventeen years as chairman and CEO of American Express, everyone knew Jim and everyone returned his calls. He retired from American Express in 1994 and founded RRE Investors, LLC, a New York City-based VC firm. I was fortunate enough to land RRE as one of my lead investors in Evoke Software in 1996. RRE took a board seat, which they held until Evoke was acquired in 2003.

One of the best example of RRE's commitment and follow-through, and Jim's connections in the business world, came in late December 1998. We had an opportunity we had been working for several months with a national insurance company. We were expecting the deal to close before the end of the year when, on December 28, I got a call from the procurement officer I had been working with who informed me the deal had been placed on hold indefinitely and there was nothing he could do. The size of the opportunity was more than $1 million. We needed the deal to close in order to make our yearly sales numbers. I knew that Jim had relationships with some of the senior executives in the insurance company, so I called him and asked if he could help. I explained the deal on the table and pointed out that we had extended significant discounts that would expire December 31. Jim said he would see what he could do.

About an hour later, I got a call from the procurement officer who said, "I don't know what you did, but I have your signed purchase order on my desk with instructions to send it to you immediately!"

At our January board meeting, I nicknamed Jim "The Hammer" and announced that Jim Robinson III was our Salesman of the Quarter.

53. Can you be strategic?

When I was promoted to my first CEO role, I was coming from a vice president of sales position. When I met with my board and they offered me the job, one of my board members, Bob Kagle, then a partner at Technology Venture Investors (TVI) and later one of the cofounder's of Benchmark Capital, said, "My biggest concern is, can you be strategic?"

I didn't respond, I just nodded as if I understood. But actually, I didn't understand. I had no clue what he meant. But the way he made the statement scared the hell out of me. So I began my research on what it means for a CEO to be strategic. I starting calling every Silicon Valley CEO I knew, scheduling coffee and lunches and asking them "What does it mean to you to be strategic?"

After about six months of research, and speaking with at least twenty other CEOs, I had twenty different answers. I got responses such as developing long-range financial plans to increasing deal size with more expensive products. One great example came from a CEO who said, "If I sell you $1 million worth of paperclips, then I am your strategic paperclip supplier." It took a while before I really knew and understood what it meant to be strategic, and it was actually a combination of all of the answers I got from my twenty CEO friends.

Here is what my answer to What does it mean to be strategic is today:

It's being aware of and understanding the challenges to achieving long-term sustainable growth and having execution plans to address those challenges. It means building and offering products and services that are critical to your customers so that their long-term success is dependent on your company delivering those products and services to them. It means your company is of critical importance to your customer's success strategy.

54. Managing a board of directors.

I've had the opportunity to mentor a number of CEOs over the years, and one of the areas they all seemed to struggle with is learning to manage their board of directors, although it is one of the most critical factors in their careers. While it's true some board members are difficult to manage, it can be done.

A few rules I subscribe to are as follows.

- Never surprise any board member with information during the board meeting, even if it's a good surprise. Have a one on one with every board member before the board meeting to review your agenda, review quarterly results, and prepare them for any disappointing news.

- Know before the meeting what each member will or won't support. Align your allies and be sure you have enough support for your ideas. If you don't, leave it off the agenda.

- Do your best to keep items not on the agenda from coming up. Such discussions can go in any direction, and you can quickly lose control.

- Thoroughly review and approve all presentations that you allow your management team to give. Drill them on staying on topic and critique their presentation afterward. If you have someone who does not stay in line or repeatedly goes too long, don't allow them to present to the board again.

- Position every management team member to look their best.

- Control your chief financial officer (CFO) and what they present. The two of you must be in lockstep.

- Never let anyone present anything that is not 100 percent accurate.

- Your forecast must be conservative. Use written probabilities with all aspects of a forecast.

- When a board member makes a suggestion, let them see you write it down. Call them the day after the meeting and discuss it.

- Run the meeting with a tight fist, stay on the agenda, cut off anyone who goes on too long (even board members), and re-direct the conversation when needed.

55. Getting through difficult times requires everyone to pull together.

At XA Systems, a few quarters after a disastrous acquisition we were forced to make a drastic reduction in force. The number of people we would have to layoff was 115. I gathered the management team that would be needed to turn things around in Chicago to figure out what we had to do and build an execution plan for survival, including deciding what positions we would have to cut.

I started the meeting by saying these are very challenging and difficult times and to get through them everyone must pull together and focus on leading the company in a positive direction so we could quickly get back on track. I also said there will be a time to do a complete post mortem on what went wrong but now is not that time, so everyone get with the program and let's move ahead.

As soon as I had finished saying that, two managers who had come over as part of the acquisition spoke up and started attacking me for not listening to them, saying I was to blame for things not going well, and if I had followed their recommendations we wouldn't be where we were. I didn't say anything. I ignored their comments and redirected the meeting to the challenge at hand and started focusing on how we would carry out the layoff, how to determine what positions would need to be on the cut list, and so on. But before I did that, I leaned over to my CFO, who was sitting next to me and, on his note pad wrote the number 115, drew a line through it, and next to it wrote 117. That was Saturday morning. Before everyone left for home that evening, I terminated the two managers who spoke up and ignored my instructions to move forward in a constructive and positive direction.

Surviving difficult times requires that your entire team be on board, that everyone is on the same page, and that everyone is pulling together. If not, make the changes necessary to get everyone aligned and focused. If there are some who refuse to move ahead constructively, fire them.

56. Founder's disease.

There are many great companies you've heard of where the CEO leading the company was not the founder. There are several other companies you have not heard of, but should have, where the founder is still running the company. It is rare that the founding CEO takes a company to high levels of success. There are exceptions of course, such as Oracle, Salesforce.com, and Amazon. But it's more common for the founder to turn the company over to an executive experienced in building and growing a company.

Often when a promising company is not growing as expected, the founding CEO attempts to hire a CEO but wants to stay involved in the company. That seldom works, due to the founder meddling and wanting to exercise too much control. An experienced CEO will not tolerate that and won't stay around long. Then the founder hires another CEO and the cycle repeats. Only when the founder fully steps aside, relinquishes control, and allows an experienced CEO to take control and run the company can the company begin to realize its potential. This scenario is why when VC-backed companies decide it's time for new leadership, the founder/CEO is almost never allowed to stay around.

In the mid-1990s, Unison Software was a fourteen-year-old company that had peaked at $14 million in annual sales. There was an offer on the table to acquire the company for $14 million. Instead of selling the company for one time revenue, Don Lee, the founder/CEO offered me the position of President and COO with a promise to let me run the company. I was skeptical, but decided to give it a try. I knew the company was in a good position and poised to grow rapidly with the right execution.

True to his word, Don gave me the control to do what I needed to do and let me do the job he hired me to do. I completely revamped the sales teams in the U.S. and Europe and hired a new director of product development. Sales grew by 50 percent the first year and, on my first anniversary date with the company, I was on an IPO road show. The company valuation at the close of the first day of trading was almost $80 million, exactly one year after the $14 million acquisition offer. Two years later, Unison was acquired by Tivoli/IBM for $170 million.

I have met with several founder/CEOs over the years. Most were brilliant engineers with innovative technology and promising market potential, but their companies were unable to get adequate sales traction. In many of those situations, it was obvious to me the reason for that was the person I was meeting with. Their characteristics were common. They were typically very passionate about their product and company, often not adequately funded because the VC community wanted to see more sales revenue, and they complained loudly about their inability to find and keep good sales execs and reps.

Of the required skills needed to be a successful entrepreneurial CEO, they possessed few. I could see that without new, experienced leadership the desired traction would not likely come.

57. Never let anything cause you to compromise your honesty and integrity. No matter what the motivation, it will not be worth it.

Honesty is habit forming. So is dishonesty. The first time someone lies to hide something will make the second time they do it easier. Misreporting financial data, even by a little, could cost you your credibility and maybe even your job. And if your company is publicly traded, even your freedom.

In business, not being able to trust your sources for data on operations is unacceptable. The world is way too full of smart people who know immediately when they are not getting a straight answer. Once you get tagged as someone who can't be trusted, you may never recover.

This harkens back to the saying, "Most people are not smart enough to lie. But if by chance you are, then you don't need to."

58. As an entrepreneur you are a risk taker, not a gambler.

One of the differences between an entrepreneur and a gambler is that an entrepreneur has a considerable amount of control over the factors that determine the outcome, while a gambler has very little control over those factors. An entrepreneur who does their homework, does enough detailed planning, and manages their optimism well enough can have a good shot at success, as long as they don't stop learning along the way.

59. Everything takes longer than you think it will.

It's human nature to underestimate the amount of time and effort it will take us to do things. We all oversimplify what needs to be done and how long it will take. We assume everything will go smoothly with no disruptions or delays. That's almost never the case. It's the reason so many people are always late.

That's even more true when estimating the timing and delivery on the execution in business plans. This is no doubt the number-one reason for a company missing its planned targets.

A good rule to operate by is, "Take your most liberal esti-mate, double it, and you will still miss it by half."

60. Never bet the farm on something new or unproven.

I've done several acquisitions and launched numerous major product or market-expansion initiatives. Until I learned bet-ter, a few of those involved significant risk, putting oper-ations that were working in danger due to either spending requirements or diversion of resources.

After a particular product acquisition intended to comple-ment our current product line and increase the value of sales opportunities, we found the distraction in the sales team and an unexpectedly longer decision cycle for the new product was having a seriously negative impact on overall results. If left unaddressed, it would jeopardize the success of entire company.

Subsequently we had to suspend sales of the newly acquired product and pull out all the stops to get the sales team refo-cused on our original products. I even gave away a restored 1964½ Mustang in a "Back-to-the-Future" sales contest to the sales rep who sold the most of our old product line.

A much smarter plan would have been to launch the acquired product with a smaller, separately focused sales team until we better understood the sales process and acceptance level of the new product.

Today I consider the recurring operational success of any part of an organization sacred and not to be tampered with or put at risk. Success comes at a high cost and should never be incurred twice.

61. No one ever has just one bad quarter.

I first met Cristina Morgan in the late 1980s when she was a partner with Hambrecht and Quist, the San Francisco-based investment banker. We became friends and worked together on a number of projects over the years. She rose through the ranks through promotions and company acquisitions and is today vice chairman of investment banking at JP Morgan Chase. She was our lead banker when we took Unison Software public. Cristina helped me fund the launch of Evoke Software as an investment banker and a personal investor. She also sat on my board for more than five years at Evoke.

Cristina taught me many things over the years, but one of the things I remember best is when, after a disappointing quarter at Evoke, I called her to prepare her for the upcoming board meeting. On the call I made the comment, "These results are from a few isolated events that we will quickly address and be back on track next quarter," to which she replied, "Lacy, no one ever has just one bad quarter."

She was, of course, right. What Cristina was saying is that when well-built plans are missed, almost always there is something fundamentally wrong, so you must figure out what that is and address it. And that is seldom a short-term fix.

62. Sometimes the most important task at hand is just survival.

After disappointing results or setbacks, when it seems your goals are out of reach, taking a step back and focusing on a set of short-term achievable objectives may help get things back under control and give you a chance to fight another day. Those objectives should be based just on what it will take to survive. Accomplishing anything that gets you closer to knowing you are on your way back can be uplifting. Once things are in hand, then you can revisit your higher goals from a position of stability.

But first thing first: Secure your survival.

63. The only unforgivable sin in business is running out of cash.

Starting, building, and growing a company will present a significant number of challenges. You can recover from many of those challenges, however, by staying on top of things and addressing them quickly. There is one exception, and that is running out of cash.

When a company runs out of cash, recovery is almost impossible. When that happens, things falls apart and usually very quickly. Credit lines are canceled, loans are called, accounts are closed, staff stops working because they're not getting paid, foreclosures start, and the list goes on.

Of all of the responsibilities of a CEO, none is as important as ensuring the company is adequately financed. It's also usually the most difficult. Conservative, detailed planning with contingencies must always be in place and kept up-to-date.

One of the biggest dangers for early-stage companies is that entrepreneurs are optimistic, otherwise they probably wouldn't be entrepreneurs. They want to believe the best news and want to think that good things are going to happen. Unfortunately, even when the good things do happen, they almost always take longer than expected.

If you are managing a venture-backed company that is running out of cash and you are able to get financing from your current investors, it is likely to be the most expensive money you will ever get. When you have no other options, your risk profile will mean giving up substantial equity for a chance at survival. I've seen bridge loans with terms that result in 90 percent of a company's equity going to the funding parties. But when you're only choices are that or failure, there is not much else you can do.

So the *Takeaway* here is plan ahead carefully, manage your expectations, tightly control spending, cut costs before you have to, and have a backup plan. In other words, never run out of cash!

64. You make money by selling your products, not by building build them.

Selling your product is typically much more difficult than building it is. No one is lying awake at night trying to think of ways to prevent you from building your product, but there are countless people lying awake trying to think of ways to stop you from selling it. Those people are called competitors.

Having the best product is a godsend for a sales team, but in no way guarantees success. The dream scenario is having a brilliant engineering team who thoroughly understands what customers want and need and builds products that address those wants and needs. Then having a sales and marketing team partner cooperatively with the engineers so they all work together for mutual success.

Companies don't usually fail because they can't build a great product. It's more common to fail because they couldn't sell it or, more specifically, couldn't sell enough of it fast enough.

65. Selling to wants versus needs.

I once had a young lady named Jamie who regularly cut my hair. The salon where she worked frequently had sales contests for their employees to encourage them to sell more hair products. The most successful employee could win items like dinner for two at a local restaurant, a bottle of wine, and so on.

I offered to help Jamie develop a sales pitch for selling hair products to her customers. I explained to her that needs are a basic reaction to a given situation, that is, I need a new pair of shoes because mine are falling apart. Wants are an emotional response, that is, I want a new pair of shoes because the pair I see in the window are attractive.

Not so ironically, humans are more driven by our wants than our needs. The sales pitch we developed for Jamie was for her to sell to wants. As she was washing a customer's hair she would say, "This shampoo makes your hair look great. You're going to want to take some home with you. You're going to love how you look." As she was finishing with the customer, she reached for a bottle of the hair product and handed it to the customer, again saying, "You really will love this."

Jamie never lost a salon sales contest from then on and often sold two to three times what any other employee sold.

It's a little more difficult in the business world to sell to wants, but it is certainly not impossible. If your product can help someone be more successful, that is definitely something they want. Positioning it that way may help get an emotional decision, which is more likely to stick.

66. It's better to have too many controls than to have too few. You can relax them over time. An out-of-control business is hard to fix.

Like it or not, people need controls and guidelines to guide them in decision-making. There must be limitations placed on everyone. Without the proper controls and guidelines, there can be inconsistencies that result in ineffective operations that may, at a minimum, limit an organization's ability to achieve its potential. This is especially true when it comes to decision-making regarding spending and the allocation of financial resources.

People will often make decisions with too little regard for how those decisions affect others outside their sphere or the impact they can have on the organization as a whole. Guidelines and controls are the only way to manage that.

Limitations on spending and decision-making are necessary to avoid people making decisions in isolation. An organization must have in place proper oversight to ensure consistency and healthy growth.

67. The shorter the time period for measuring progress, the more control you have.

The British actor and comedian, John Cleese, in one of his corporate training videos, tells the story of his favorite toy growing up. It was Gordon the Guided Missile. He said that Gordon was always off course and had to make course corrections every few seconds, otherwise he would miss his target by miles. He went on to say that the only time Gordon was exactly on course was when he was just a few seconds from his target.

I'm not suggesting that anyone monitor and course-correct every few seconds, unless you are building and firing guided missiles. But for the rest of us, there is likely a frequency that makes sense that will allow you to see actual progress and make adjustments accordingly.

This fits with the philosophy that plans are not necessarily built to be right. You build them so you will know when you are off course and can quickly make corrections and get back on course. At least that's what Gordon the Guided Missile says.

68. Every company has its own unique economic formula that will determine its degree of success or its failure.

There is an economic formula in effect in every company, whether the company knows it or not. These are the inter-related factors that determine the outcome and results of the company's operations. Any company that doesn't know what its economic formula is needs to figure it out, determine how it's working, and discover what can be done to make it work better.

This came to light for me early in my first CEO role at XA Systems. I was going through one of my first annual planning sessions with my leadership team trying to figure out what the key operational elements were and how to optimize their effect on our results. I came to realize that the effect each component had on the other components had to be considered before we could optimize our operating plan.

For example, engineering cost allocation, depending on which of our products we invested in, would affect product pricing, the length of the sales cycle, the cost of sales, competitive positioning, product support cost, presales effort and cost, maintenance and enhancement pricing, and so on. We had to decide if it was better to enhance our products to shorten the sales cycle, increase product pricing, or integrate products so we could increase average deal size.

Another example was if we invested in the number of sales-team members, would that have more of an effect than if we increased the number of pre-sales support team members or increased marketing program spending. And those decisions were affected by product-enhancements decisions as well as new-product-development decisions.

It became apparent that we first had to identify all of the operational factors, then figure out how each affected the others. The goal was to optimize how they all worked together to produce the optimum growth and profitability results.

Identifying the key components of a company's economic formula is not an easy exercise. Determining how they affect each other is even more challenging, made more difficult by the fact there is never just one right answer.

This time-consuming exercise helps you visualize all of the inter-working components that determine your company's results. Figuring out what those components are and their effect on each other will give you the ability to have maximum impact on your operational planning, effectiveness, and your company's performance.

69. Don't wait until it's too late to get desperate.

You've got to know when a sense of urgency is just not enough. A leader must know when and how to hit the panic button to achieve its maximum effect. If you are heading toward a situation where you are going to be fighting for your life, the sooner you recognize that the more likely you are to survive.

The key to knowing when to get desperate is having your finger on all of the key metrics that will determine your outcome. Typically, those can be narrowed down to a handful of items such as cash on hand, accounts-receivables status, borrowing capacity, the reliability of sales forecasts, spending controls and policies, and the timing of execution plans for cost cutting measures, to name a few.

If your company develops complex products, accurate product-delivery schedules may play an important role in surviving a desperate situation. Reliable expectations from engineering can sometimes be difficult to get. I've had to invoke daily updates on detailed, specific deliverables at times to keep up the pressure.

One frustrating phenomenon that can happen is with sales forecasting. If you put pressure on a sales team because their original forecast falls short of what's required, invariably the sales team will increase the forecasted numbers, although little will have changed to cause sales-opportunity results to change. In my experience, pressuring a sales team to increase performance in the short term seldom works.

The important point here is to know exactly where you are, have your fingers on the pulse of all the key items, and get everyone fired up soon enough to make enough of a difference.

70. A solid strategy versus errors in execution.

A company's strategy must include a well-defined market opportunity and an accompanying execution plan that takes full advantage of that opportunity. These two critical components must be frequently revisited to ensure they remain correct. The follow on to that is making sure your key operational managers fully understand both.

During a period of rapid growth at one of my companies, because we had promoted and hired a number of new managers, I knew the opportunity for operational mistakes was high. To try and minimize that, I gathered the entire management team together and we built what we called our company's strategic framework. We took our market opportunity and broke it down into meaningful components that were uniquely relevant to each department.

We then built detailed strategic plans by department, along with matching execution plans directly tied to each department's objectives. We created a framework chart for each management team member with a list of specific actions that, if focused on, would keep them well within the strategic framework and keep everyone going in the same direction.

I directed the team to revisit their framework charts several times each day so that, as they made decisions and gave directions, the consistency and focus toward accomplishing our common goals would be assured.

Although I knew there would still be errors in execution, as long as our strategy remained solid and everyone understood it, with the level of consistent guidance we provided we would still achieve our goals.

71. Plans are nothing. Planning is everything. —*General Dwight Eisenhower*

The purpose of a plan is not to be right. The purpose of a plan is to give you the tools to measure your progress over time and be a guide to help keep you on track so you can make the adjustments you need to make to meet your end goal.

The message General Eisenhower was sending was that a detailed planning process will familiarize you so well with all of the elements of your operation that, when adjustments need to be made, you will be equipped with the detailed knowledge and know what must be adjusted to keep you on course.

72. Use your legal counsel to keep you out of trouble, not get you out of trouble.

It's tempting for an entrepreneur to believe they can do everything, even try to interpret potentially litigious situations and assess legal exposure, but that's a high-risk way to operate. The time to engage a lawyer is before you need one.

It is true that legal advice can be expensive and lawyers have certainly been known to over-complicate matters, but seeking sound legal advice at the right time can be the difference between spending your time building a strong business versus spending your time building a strong legal defense.

73. Don't allow the existence of a sales-prevention department

I've closed thousands of sales contracts in my career. Many have been challenging to negotiate and painful to close. Some customers, especially procurement officers, can be difficult, but I've never failed to get a license agreement or sales contract through that process.

One reason that effort has been successful is that I have always tried to prevent the formation of a sales-prevention department within my own company. Unfortunately, I was not always successful.

At one of my companies, although I was President, the CFO did not report to me. The founder held on to that function and the CFO reported to him. To say the CFO did not have a grasp on sales was a gross understatement. He completely missed the point when it came to knowing how to help get a deal closed. It was so bad that it was well-recognized among our sales team that getting the customer to buy was often easier than getting a deal through our own finance department.

If sales-prevention departments arise, they can destroy a company. When well-meaning, strong, ego-driven people who lack a basic understanding of how deals get done are given too much control, they can destroy morale and kill months of progress. Allowing them to continue can severely harm a company.

74. Your CFO does not run the company. Don't let them act like they do.

Good financial executives are, by nature, heavily control oriented. And that's a good thing. Any good accounting manager, controller, or CFO needs to be detail-focused and always seeking answers to questions when something does not look the way it should. They also need to ensure the CEO is aware if policies and procedures are not being followed, knows beforehand when spending levels are headed for trouble, and numerous other vital financial data points.

The problem comes when the CFO also believes it's their responsibility to fix those problems. And that happens a lot. I've had my own CFO attempt to take on that role and have observed several other CFOs do the same thing. I've seen them brutally beat up their peer executives, creating serious morale problems, even to the point of other VPs threatening to resign. Allowed to perpetuate, others in the company can lose respect for the CEO and start viewing the CFO as the person who really runs the company and the one whose approval they must seek. Unfortunately, many CEOs stand by and allow that to happen.

A competent CFO is hard to find. A competent CFO who partners well with their peers and has a supportive, helpful attitude is even more difficult to find. Of the nine or ten CFOs I've employed, I would put only two in the latter category.

75. Increasing your average deal size can dramatically accelerate growth.

When it comes to finding ways to accelerate growth, if you can increase your deal size without extending the sales cycle or increasing the cost of sales, you can make remarkable progress quickly.

In all of my companies, I drive home the philosophy that when you're in a deal, sell them all of your products they will ever need while you are there. I've often said to my sales team, "Keep giving them software until you get all of their money."

The pushback that you are cannibalizing future revenue opportunities misses the mark. The cost of sales is often two to three times the cost of product development. No one should incur the cost of sales twice for the same product for the same customer. Applying this philosophy, you will get more money and you will get it sooner. Then you can use the additional cash to develop new products, then go back and sell them those.

The resulting impact that larger deal sizes will have on growth can be dramatic. And if managed correctly, there will be no increase in the length of the sales cycle. If your sales management is skilled at closing large enterprise deals, the difference in closing $100,000 deals versus $500,000 deals can be managed with no change in the time it takes in getting them closed.

76. Build products that help you to sell more, charge more, sell faster.

I've asked my product-planning and engineering teams many times, "Unless the products we are building results in allowing us to sell more, charge more, or sell faster, why are we building them?"

Breaking those three challenges down, sell more relates to expanding product capabilities to address a broader market opportunity, resulting in having more customers to sell to.

Allowing us to charge more means the results of the product-development effort will make the product more valuable to our customers so they will pay more for it.

Sell faster is almost always related to ease of use. Products that are easy to implement, easy to learn, and easy to use will get bought faster. And that has a multiplying productivity factor. The quicker a product is purchased, the shorter the sales cycle, the lower the cost of sales, and the more time sales will have to sell to other customers.

77. Listen to your prospects more closely than to your customers.

This is not to say don't listen to your customers. Of course you should. The care and feeding of your customer base is vital.

But your future will be determined more by those who have not yet bought from you than those who already have.

Serious mistakes can be made when markets progress and move to newer technologies and products. However large they are, installed base customers are often slow to move and their demand for support and upgrades to older products can be significant.

Don't let spending too much on older products for current customers cause you to fall behind the competition and where the market is moving. True innovation usually comes from newly developed products, not from upgrades to old ones. And that's what customers who have not already bought older editions want.

Your current customers may not want or need the new products anytime soon, because what they bought from you two years ago is still good enough. But your future depends on new customer sales. Falling behind advancing technology and moving market trends could make catching up difficult.

78. One of the hardest things for an entrepreneur to do is call it quits.

If you are not an optimist, you would not likely be an entrepreneur. But with that optimism comes a bit of a blind side when trying to objectively evaluate your chances of success. Obviously, success requires drive, determination, and a willingness to keep going when others may give up. But continuing to press on when your realistic chances of a successful outcome are too low is not the thing to do.

With the help of an experienced outside confidant, develop a reality test and commit beforehand to abide by the results. Good money after bad and all those other sayings are quoted for a reason.

79. When you have done your best and all the cards are on the table, don't be afraid to walk away.

At Indicative Software, in 2007 we were competing for the largest deal in company history and had reached the final-negotiation stage. The customer was the largest Internet service provider in Europe, with headquarters in London. Their technical teams and most of the company staff were based in Paris. We made a significant investment in the opportunity and had sent engineering and support team members to Paris several times to scope out the requirements and put together our proposed solution. I traveled to London and Paris several times during the competition as well. We put together a detailed, comprehensive, and aggressive proposal and had our best team on the project, led by John Smith, the founder of Indicative and the person who knew more about our product and the market space than anyone. We went to great lengths to defend our technology and our product, and to construct a thorough and complete proposal.

The competition came down to two finalists, Indicative Software, a company based in Fort Collins, Colorado, with around 100 employees, and IBM. We were called to London to present our proposal and our competitor, IBM, was called in to present as well. We were told they would present the day before us.

The price for our solution was well over a million dollars. After spending the better part of the day presenting and defending our proposal, we were told that IBM had offered to cut their price substantially and our proposal was now considerably higher. We were asked to think it over and come back with our best and final. Both John Smith and I knew we had a good solution and felt it was probably better than what IBM had proposed, but we did not know that for sure.

I remember sitting and staring at the purchasing manager, who was negotiating for the customer and letting my stare linger and get uncomfortable after she had asked us to think it over and come back with a better price. After several minutes I said, "We believe our solution is the best you will find and that it is worth what we are asking. You have our best price. We cannot go any lower."

We were politely ushered out of the office and headed back to our hotel. When I got back to my room, I got a phone call from the chief information officer (CIO), who was in charge of the evaluation for the customer telling me that our proposal had been accepted.

Several times in my career, when I was convinced that our proposal was as solid as any solution available and our price was fair, I have refused to lower the price.

In all of those customer opportunities, I made sure we built excellent relationships with all of the key influencers up and down the organization. I personally developed and managed a number of those relationships myself.

Fortunately, my teams and I have never lost when we did that.

80. Your first 100 customers will teach you how to build your company if you listen carefully to them.

When we launched Evoke Software, the effort actually stared with a company that had been around a while and was in its second or third iteration without much traction.

I asked Julie Lane, whom I had worked with at XA Systems and Unison Software, to join me in helping to build Evoke. Julie was highly skilled at selling large deals and closing business, which is exactly what was needed.

Our product was quite complex and solved a serious problem. However, most customers did not even know there was a solution, which presented a big challenge to creating a successful go-to-market strategy. But once we got a customer to listen to our story, understand our approach to addressing the challenge. and fully appreciate what we had to offer, we could often convince them to buy. The problem was that sometimes that could take several months. However we had no choice except to go through that learning process. Until Julie and I had enough experience with the customer's evaluation processes, their decision-making cycles, and financial justifications, we really didn't know how to build a successful sales strategy.

It took listening to and learning from our first 100 customers for us to fine-tune the sales and marketing programs that enabled us to really begin to build and grow the company. With every new customer, we learned as much as we could and continued to focus on getting smarter with every success.

It eventually worked, and the length of our sales cycles went from six to nine months to three to four months.

DECISION-MAKING

81. Every time you decide to do something you are, in effect, deciding not to do several other things.

This comes down to the simple rule that you can't have everything and you can't do everything. So, when you make decisions about where to spend your time or where to spend your money, each decision will logically eliminate several other options. This comes into play in a significant way when it comes to budgeting and planning, but it can be an even more impactful rule to consider in day-to-day operations. Getting your team to think that way every time they spend company money can have a big effect. But it's not easy to teach that to some people to the point where they internalize it and consistently operate that way.

I had a vice president of sales at one of my companies who was one of the most talented relationship managers I've ever known. I observed him close a half-million-dollar deal with a CIO who had never seen the product. He made the decision based solely on the trusted relationship he had with my VP. But the VP also had a few downsides when it came to decision-making. He didn't always think things through.

Not long after moving into a new headquarters office, I came to work one morning to find a large new lamp in the lobby. I asked our office manager where it came from and she told me the VP of sales had bought it, using his company credit card. I could tell it was expensive. I went to the VP's office, pointed out that it was not his responsibility to purchase office furniture, and asked how much the lamp cost. As I suspected, it cost more than a thousand dollars.

I then had my assistant go through the sales budget and identify several line items where the expense was similar to the cost of the lamp. I sent the list of those items to the VP and had him choose which to eliminate.

The point I was making is that every dollar spent must be viewed from the perspective of a trade-off you are making. The power of this rule when it comes to discretionary spending can be significant.

82. Make decisions slowly. Carry them out swiftly. Don't look back.

Many situations, if left alone, can resolve themselves. By being patient, calm, observant, and asking questions, the best solution may become obvious to everyone. But if a decision is required, always wait until it needs to be made, then execute on it swiftly, move ahead forcefully, and do not revisit it nor allow anyone else to do so.

The exception is if new information comes to light that was not previously known and could have a material impact on the results. But even then, seriously consider any disruptions that a change in course may have and be certain that doing it is the right thing.

Second-guessing yourself after a decision is made can show a lack of confidence and may be seen by others as weak leadership. In many situations, there is not just one correct decision. There are probably a number of actions that could work. It comes down to making the one you choose work. If others question your decision, it's okay to listen, but unless critical new information has come forward, continue to move ahead and make your decision work. Don't hesitate to say, "I appreciate your input, but the decision is made and this is what we're going to do."

83. The higher your authority and responsibility level, the fewer decisions you should make.

As you rise in authority and responsibility, you may expect to be making more decisions. If you're wise, that won't be the case. It's better to push decisions down to the person who has the most information and knowledge about the situation as well as being responsible for carrying out the implementation. As an added advantage, you also have the opportunity to tie accountability and ownership more directly to the people responsible for making the decision and managing the results.

84. Good analytics are important, but they cannot replace good judgment.

Numbers don't lie is a legendary saying that cannot be forgotten. But numbers often don't tell the whole story. A thorough analysis using sophisticated analytics is an important input into serious, high-stakes decision making. Not doing that can be fatal. But analytics cannot replace judgment.

We all know about analysis paralysis and have no doubt seen it. That usually occurs when no one with good judgment is involved or leading the process and someone is waiting for analytics to reveal the one best answer. If that's possible, then good. But in many cases, it doesn't happen that way.

Experience and knowledge are required to do effective analysis. But to interpret the analytics as well as factor in the numerous additional considerations and make a good decision requires good judgment.

A good example of this *Takeaway* is mergers and acquisitions (M&A) transactions. There is certainly no shortage of data to analyze during the due-diligence phase of a transaction. Anything and everything meaningful is made available, and the time allowed to perform whatever analytics desired is allotted. Seldom is time pressure a significant factor.

So with all of that data to study, the number of smart people available to perform endless sophisticated analytics, and the extensive market analysis and research typically completed, why is it that, according to *Harvard Business Review*, between 70 and 90 percent of all M&A transactions fail?

There are countless books written on the subject if you want to better understand this paradox, but could it be that because the stakes are so high, there is too much reliance on analytics and not enough reliance on judgment?

Let me repeat this *Takeaway*:

Good analytics are important, but cannot replace good judgment.

Any go/no-go decision on an M&A transaction will come down to someone making a judgment call. Perhaps that is something worth studying.

85. Success teaches you what to do under a given set of circumstances that will never occur again. Failure will teach you a thousand things to never do again.

Most statistics show first time entrepreneurs have an 18 percent success rate while second-time entrepreneurs who previously failed have a 30 percent success rate.

My first significant acquisition turned out to be a dismal failure. We almost lost our entire company, and six months into it we had to lay off a third of our staff. Looking back, the lessons learned from that experience could fill volumes. However, that failure has paid tremendous dividends since.

Had it succeeded, it is possible a subsequent acquisition could have been an even more spectacular failure. With the lessons from that failure, I learned much more about the hard questions that need to be asked and the numerous risks that must be assessed, the kind of lessons that can only come from experience. And that's not even mentioning the pain caused by that failure, which I never want repeated.

86. Good data is necessary to make good decisions, but use data wisely. If you use it to punish people, you will stop getting good data.

I've sat in meetings and watched leaders ask for and receive critical information on engineering projects, sales forecasts, product-delivery schedules, financial-reporting deadlines, and numerous other operational details, and then watched as the leader flew into a rage because they didn't hear what they wanted to hear. I've also observed those same leaders fed lines of total B.S. by managers and operational staff because they didn't want to get yelled at for telling the truth.

One of the first lessons I learned as a CEO was to get the bad news first and get it as soon as it was available. If that happened, maybe I would have time to react and do something about it.

Punishing the people who give you the information you need most does not make sense. No one should ever feel threatened because they are willing to tell the truth.

87. Be sure you are listening to the right person. Don't be manipulated by someone with a hidden agenda.

Be cautious and wise when getting advice, especially unsolicited advice. The higher you go in an organization and the more responsibility you have, the more people will want to influence you. Never forget that many people have an agenda that may not be in line with you or your company's best interest.

Many times, it may be clear that someone is trying to manipulate you. But when someone wants you to do something that affects others, either for good or bad, be sure you have all the relevant facts before taking action.

I had a telemarketing manager who frequently lobbied against a marketing programs manager, complaining about how ineffective he was and that he should be replaced. Although the case against him was highly subjective, eventually he was replaced.

Later I found out that a previous relationship between a close friend of the telemarketing manager and the marketing programs manager had ended badly. After his dismissal, the telemarketing manager confided in someone who then told me that she really wanted the marketing programs manager fired because of how he treated her friend.

BE A SMART OPERATOR

88. When you take a new management or leadership position, withhold your judgment and make no changes for at least thirty days and no major changes for at least ninety days.

When coming into a new position, you know very little about the situation, regardless of what you have been told. It's best to keep your mouth shut and your eyes and ears open for at least thirty days. Ask lots of questions and learn as much as you can. Also, the more questions you ask, the higher your personal credibility will be. Keep your early opinions to yourself. We all know that opinions formed too quickly are often wrong. Don't be quick to pass judgment on people or how things get done.

When I have taken over an organization, many of the opinions I formed during the first thirty days were very different ninety days later.

When I took over as CEO of Indicative Software, one of our marketing team members was a person who answered questions with excruciating detail. He was so detail oriented that I would quickly get lost in what he was saying and found speaking with him to be practically useless. One of my main tasks was to reduce spending, and that would likely involve a headcount reduction. But I knew enough to reserve judgment on people.

After my learning curve started to flatten, I eventually began to comprehend more of what he was saying. I specifically remember the day I said to him, "Larry, you really talk a lot, but you also say a lot."

He turned out to be one of our most valuable assets in charting our course through some complex product-development and product-marketing challenges. Withholding my judgment allowed Indicative to build around a key team member who made a significant contribution. Passing judgment quickly would have cost us that contribution.

89.   The problem with Yes Men: When two people always agree, one of them is unnecessary.

One of the keys to sustained and repeatable success is to surround yourself with people who make you better, make you think of things you may not have thought of on your own, are smarter that you, have expertise you don't have, and are not afraid to disagree with you.

Building such a team is difficult, and it takes a leader who is confident, self-assured, and not easily threatened. It takes someone who leads by asking questions and openly seeks input and guidance from others.

It's important to build a culture where your team is encouraged to respectfully disagree with each other as well. Collective intelligence can be a powerful force, but you only get that when you and your leadership team can have constructive disagreements and everyone's ideas are given airtime.

When two smart people disagree on an important topic, it can often lead to better decisions being made.

90. Never allow yourself to own someone else's problems.

Being empathetic is an admirable trait. But that does not mean taking ownership of someone else's problems. You definitely are not doing anyone or yourself justice by doing so. We all have to own and solve our own problems.

Several years ago, I took a class called Monkey Training. The objective of the class was to develop skills and awareness so you never left a meeting or even a conversation with someone else's monkey on your back.

Years later, I was asked to meet with a senior support engineer to review a problem we were having with one of our customers. He went into extreme detail about the problem and I finally figured out he expected me to solve it. It would have taken me a long time, and I was already very busy. I finally said, "Walter, I am not going to do this." That's all I said. I then left the meeting.

I did tell our manager about the conversation to be sure I wasn't out of line. He had a good laugh and said he would handle it. I never heard anything else about it.

91. Mediocre talent in key roles can be fatal.

If you have team full of average performers that you call successful, it's a joke and you are the punch line.

No company will ever fill its ranks with superstars, but in certain key roles superstars should be your minimum acceptable criteria. Figure out which 25 percent of your positions needs to be occupied by the very best and staff accordingly.

This is not a lesson we learn early in our careers. As you develop new leaders, use the performance standard of having at least 25 percent of their team being superstars to elevate the performance standards they need to have for their teams.

Most new leaders will look for and judge their team and themselves on a meets-the-requirements level of performance. That is the attitude of someone whose goal is to finish the race. You want to develop leaders who want to not just finish the race but win the race. You will need a few star performers to do that.

92. Recognition can be a good thing, until you start believing your own press.

In my first few years as CEO at XA Systems, I was fortunate enough to get a number of awards and receive lots of recognition. We placed XA in the Inc 500 for two years in a row, one of the first companies to do that. I was a featured CEO in an issue of *Inc Magazine*, I was chosen CEO of the year by *Insider Magazine*, I was invited to be the keynote speaker at several events, I was frequently interviewed by trade journals, newspapers, and the *Wall Street Journal*, and the list grew. That was also about the time I made several aggressive growth decisions that turned out to be bad decisions.

Clearly, my ego was out of control. I felt invincible, and operated as if I could do no wrong. Looking back after things began to fall apart, I could see huge holes in my logic behind some of those decisions.

But I made them because I was convinced I was right. I used to wonder why no one on my management team or my board stepped up and tried to talk some sense into me or question my decisions. But I know why they didn't. They knew I wouldn't have listened to them anyway.

We all enjoy being recognized for our successful efforts and hard work. But no matter what good things others may say about us, we are still capable of screwing things up.

93. Be absolutely certain you know who controls the power if you are planning a rebellion.

> Things may not be the way you think they are or the way the organizational structure implies it is.
>
> I once watched a colleague self-destruct by not accurately interpreting who really had the power and influence in our company. In this case, he went above our manager's head to the next-level senior manager to complain about our direct manager. He badly misread the power structure. After complaining to his boss's boss, his boss immediately fired him.
>
> It was obvious to me who really had the power, and I knew exactly what was going to happen. I figured out what he was planning and even called and cautioned him against it. But he didn't listen. What he was complaining about was legitimate, but had nothing to do with the outcome.
>
> Just because a reporting structure indicates who is in charge, it doesn't always mean that's how the real power flows.

94. Confiding in someone you trust and respect who is not directly involved can be valuable.

> Many times in our lives, often prompted by a question from someone not directly involved with work or with another challenge we are facing, we hear ourselves say something we didn't know we were thinking. We pause and say to ourselves, *I didn't realize that is what I thought, but it's exactly what I needed to hear.*

Seek an uninvolved party you trust and engage them is a discussion on a topic that is challenging you. Our brain is working non-stop to solve our problems. Sometimes we just need to give it a chance to tell us what it has come up with.

95. It's not who you know ... it's who knows you.

From 2008 until 2012, I was executive chairman of John Moores Equity, the private equity and holding company owned by John Moores. John was the founder of BMC Software; owner of the San Diego Padres Major League Baseball team; chairman of the board of the Carter Center, President Jimmy Carter's philanthropy organization; and chairman of the University of California Board of Regents, just to name a few of his roles. Needless to say, there were few people who did not know John.

I was directly responsible for nine software companies in the JME portfolio. By using John's name, there was almost no one our team could not get in to see. And if an opportunity was material enough, John was more than willing to make a call or even attend a meeting himself.

How many times have you heard someone say, "Sure, I know him/her", then you ask if they will introduce you and you never hear back.

There is usually a big difference between the number of people you know and the number of people who know you. Unless you are famous for some reason, the number in the first category will likely be much larger.

MANAGING THE DOWNSIDE

96. Sometimes you may be smarter than your teachers, bosses, and leaders, but you have to learn to deal with them without committing career suicide.

My daughter Sara reminded me that I said that to her when she was in middle school. I said it to Sara because it was true for her and it is true for countless others. Learning to accept and graciously deal with someone in control when you may be smarter than they are is a valuable lesson to learn.

It can be frustrating to have to take direction from someone when you are always a step ahead, but if you want to survive you have to treat them with respect. The smartest course of action is to be supportive, defend them, be loyal, and be their friend. Never talk down to them or speak poorly of them to others.

I reported to a gentleman once who was a senior vice president that reported to the CEO. He was a nice guy and I sincerely liked him, but he didn't have everything the job required. People who reported to me often questioned his value and each time they did I defended him, saying you don't know all the things he does so do not speak disparagingly of him.

Even his peers questioned his ability to do the job. But I was never disrespectful toward him. After about a year and a half, the board decided to make a leadership change. The VP was fired, the CEO was asked to step aside, and I was chosen as the new CEO, moving up two executive levels at once, a move almost unheard of.

One of the reasons I was offered the CEO position is that I received the support of the then-CEO and the other VPs. Later on I was told by two of the VP's that one of the reasons they felt comfortable with me assuming the CEO role is the respect I showed the fired VP while I was reporting to him, even though they knew that I was well aware of his limitations.

97. Know who you can and can't trust. Develop a keen eye for untrustworthy people. They are not hard to spot.

As a leader, you must deal in factual, accurate information. Trying to run any organization with inaccurate or incomplete data can make things much more difficult than they need to be.

I once had a regional VP of sales who had a real problem with keeping his facts straight. It wasn't obvious at first, but I kept noticing small inconsistencies and red flags in what he was telling me, so I started to double check everything I got from him.

Maintaining pricing integrity is critical for any company and one area where a bad reputation can cause irreparable harm.

After one too many pricing irregularities on contracts coming from this regional VP, I asked my controller to do an audit of all of his recent sales. What I found were several side letters offering concessions and out-clauses that violated standard, accepted revenue-recognition policies. The problem was not so far along that it couldn't be addressed but, had he been left to continue those practices, we likely would have gotten into serious trouble.

By keeping my eyes open and noticing when something didn't seem right, I was able to stop an improper business practice and prevent it from becoming an embarrassing and costly problem.

The desire and willingness to always tell the truth is simply missing for some people. In my experience, the best way to identify those you can always trust to tell you the truth is to figure out who are those you can't.

If you listen carefully to the details people give and watch for inconsistencies, you can identify those who are careless with the facts. It's not that they are necessarily bad people, because often times they are not. But as a leader, you must operate with accurate data all the time. Even slight inaccuracies can cause serious credibility issues or worse.

My advice is to find your most trustworthy team members and let them know they are part of a select group that you know will always give you the unvarnished version and that your trust in them is complete. That's paying them a high compliment, and you will probably find them stepping up and working to keep you well informed.

98. Watch out for the male ego.

The male ego has been the reason behind more lives lost, fortunes squandered, kingdoms lost, and human misery than all other reasons combined since the beginning of time. It represents the absolute worst of everything, yet also drives more success than anything.

Since this is not a history book, I'm not going to list the characters who would fall into the category described in my first sentence. You can come up with your own list anyway.

However, ego drive is an expected ingredient in all of us. We all enjoy being recognized for our contributions and successes. But an uncontrolled ego, especially an uncontrolled male ego, can be dangerous. Not surprisingly, it can drive tremendous success when combined with high intellect and talent. But if you happen to be standing too close when it explodes, you can get badly damaged or destroyed.

99. The smartest-guy-in-the-room syndrome.

Later in my career, I took a couple of positions with companies where the founder was still involved. In both cases, their company's success was each founder's first significant material wealth-creation event. Unfortunately, as can happen in these situations, the founders became convinced they were infallible. I witnessed numerous situations where they took control of a meeting when they were the least informed or least knowledgeable person in the room and begin issuing directives and edicts, never asking questions or soliciting feedback. In one situation, the founder showed up at board meetings once a quarter for forty-five minutes and conducted himself as if he was everyone's supervisor, telling them what they were doing wrong and issuing instructions. If their actions weren't so insulting to everyone there, it would have been comical.

My advice and counsel to anyone is if you think you are the smartest person is the room, almost 100 percent of the time you are wrong. You are not. You may be the one with the most authority or you may be the loudest, but you are probably not the smartest. However, should you find that you really are the smartest person in the room, my advice is to find another room.

If you find yourself in the presence of someone who is convinced of their own infallibility and believes they are the smartest one in the room, give them the room and walk away as quickly as you can.

100. The immense value of negative mentors.

I have been asked many times who were my mentors, who taught me what I know, and who were the key influences in my career. The truth is that most of the valuable lessons I learned came from working for and observing leaders who taught me what not to do. Over the years, I've worked for lying, cheating, two-faced, and unscrupulous managers. The value of seeing how destructive these people were was immensely valuable.

One of the managers I reported to early in my career used to brag about how brutal he was to others, cheating them out of sales commissions, cancelling vacation requests at the last minute, failing to approve legitimate expense reports, and numerous other nasty practices. By watching him, I became fully aware that being fair and honest in how you treat others 100 percent of the time is the only way to operate.

Watching and observing fools can teach you a lot about how not to be one.

101. You don't lose when you get knocked down. You lose when you don't get back up.

Setbacks and disappointments are facts of life we're all used to. None of us gets very far in life without blows to the body, the mind, our goals, and our dreams. We also learned that none are fatal if we keep trying.

In your career, whether you are starting and running a business or working within an organization building your success through promotions and growth in responsibilities and accountability, you are going to get knocked down.

Many knockdowns are a result of the following:

- Broken promises up the chain of authority
- Incompetent leadership
- Sabotage by a peer
- Company missteps causing a business downturn
- Trusting someone who should not have been trusted

- Taking on a challenge you were not equipped to handle
- Sexual discrimination
- Sexual harassment
- Racial or ethnic discrimination
- An event in your personal life caused you to give up
- Hostile work culture
- Male ego

For your recovery, it is vital that you identify why you were knocked down. An honest, open, and candid conversation with yourself is your first step in understanding what happened. The best result you can hope for after getting knocked down is learning from it and knowing how to prevent it from happening again.

If someone has violated your rights or broken any laws, you have every right to seek a legal remedy and no one should try to talk you out of it.

It is helpful to have a confidant whom you trust and one that has your best interests in mind.

Remember, resiliency is a key ingredient for success at anything. Take comfort in knowing knockdowns happen to everyone and that you will be wiser and better prepared for your next run at success.

FINAL THOUGHTS, THINGS TO THINK ABOUT, AND A FEW BLACKBERRY PHILOSOPHIES

- **There is probably no better productivity tool than a rolling to-do list.**

What I mean by a rolling to-do list is using a bound, journal-type notebook and each day reviewing your to-do list from yesterday, using it as an input for creating your current day's to-do list, and prioritizing all of the items according to what is most important. It may be motivational to put a few quick and easy items at the top to give yourself a feeling of accomplishment and get you off to a quick start.

I know of nothing that will keep you organized and help you prioritize better. Any busy person can get distracted, sidetracked, become unfocused, and end up wasting valuable time.

During any day, numerous interruptions can become productivity blocks. A prioritized to-do list that is visible to you at

112

all times can do wonders toward keeping you on track and getting you back on course.

Using a bound, journal-type of notebook is important because you can keep them forever. As you complete tasks, you can make notes, write down phone numbers, or make comments about what happened. I have to-do list journals going back decades, and can't count the times I've searched the past for notes, numbers, names, phone numbers, and so on that really saved my bacon.

- **Never underestimate the role of timing and luck.**

Looking back at the periods of success I've had, often I was fortunate to be at the right places at the right times to take advantage of an opportunity. In 1986, I received a call informing me the division of the company I was working for had been sold and they would be laying off almost everyone in the division and I would probably be one of them.

A few minutes after that call, my phone rang again. It was my assistant telling me I had a call from a headhunter. I typically never took calls from headhunters and she knew that, but for some reason this time she decided to ask. She was not aware of the call I'd just gotten about our division being sold.

At first I said no to the call then said, "Well, okay, put him through." When we got on the phone, the headhunter, whom I had never met or spoken with, told me about a job opportunity. A few weeks later, I ended up getting an offer and taking the job. That job a couple of years later led to my first CEO role.

After taking the job, I asked the headhunter how he found me. He said my name happened to be on a list of candidates he found in his desk, left by a former employee of the search firm for whom he was working, and something just told him to call me.

- **One of the quickest ways to lose credibility is to respond to a complex problem with a simplistic solution.**

Everyone has experienced this at some point, and you probably remember how frustrating and annoying it was. You also likely remember your opinion of the offending party when it happened and words like idiot or dumbass may have come to mind.

This *Takeaway* is be certain you fully understand the situation or problem before offering a solution. Re-read the last sentence of the preceding paragraph to fully comprehend the possible consequences of making this mistake.

- **No response is a response.**

Any time you do not get a response to a phone call, email, text, or any kind of outreach, assuming they actually got your message, the lack of a response means "You are not important enough for me to place you on my priority list of people I respond to." No matter how well-meaning the recipient may be or how regretful they may be, it means the same thing. That's still true even if they intended to respond but forgot.

If this person is someone who is important to you, accept where you stand. If, after accepting where you stand, they are still important to you, then you have work to do

- **Your feelings are not your friend.**

Our emotional response to first meeting someone is completely involuntary. We do not choose our feelings. We cannot decide if we like or dislike someone or something.

As time passes and we learn more, become more comfortable, and see and hear what others think, it can cause our feelings to change.

That is why expressing your feelings, especially the negative type, early on can have a lasting impact that you may regret.

It's likely over time that our feelings will change and we will forget how we felt. But others will not forget what we said, how they were treated, or how we made them feel.

- **A good lesson for making friends.**

When my stepson, Sulton, was in high school, he asked me for advice on how to talk with girls. There was someone he was interested in developing a closer friendship with, but he wasn't sure how to approach her. I told him that talking to a girl was the easiest thing in the world to do. And that's because you don't have to do any talking.

What I suggested is he send her a text or email asking her a question about anything with a common thread between them, such as a school assignment, a teacher they both have, or anything that two typical students would talk about. Then ask her when she will have a few minutes for you to call.

I went on to tell him, "When you are on the phone, let her begin to answer your question. When she starts talking begin to say things like 'Oh really? Tell me about that.' Then ask questions that begin with, 'How do you feel about...'? or 'What do you think about ... ?'"

In no time, Sulton's reputation among his female classmates was that he was the easiest person to talk with and they loved spending time with him.

- **You can't regret something you don't say.**

"Among my most prized possessions are the words I've never spoken."— Orson Scott Card

As difficult as it may be to hold your tongue, not responding, not engaging in a contentious discussion, or ignoring the inflammatory comments of others, is almost always the wisest thing to do.

This is especially true when the topic is your opinion of other people when that opinion is less than respectable or somewhat low. When others are offering their negative thoughts about someone else, bite your tongue. Almost certainly, someday you will be glad you did.

- **The double-edged sword of empathy.**

In the business world, especially in sales, overcoming objections is a skill that, if learned well, can make a significant difference in one's level of success. In that arena, there is little room for empathy.

But in exercising your leadership responsibility, finding the right balance between being empathetic to someone's challenges yet still requiring performance is a fine line that must be followed. Striking a balance between being a nice guy and being a hard-ass is necessary. At one time or another, you've probably worked for both types, those who leaned too far one way or the other, and you were probably frustrated by both.

What I believe is that it's best to be consistent no matter what. This will be one of those situations where how you do things is as important as what you do. Showing a complete lack of empathy is absolutely the wrong thing, but going too far the other way will backfire as well.

Your communication style as a leader can go a long way toward keeping you from falling on either of the wrong sides of empathy. What I've found is that being a good listener, asking questions to ensure understanding, showing compassion for someone's personal challenges yet still making the right business decision even if it's not what your staff member wants, will almost certainly be accepted and you will be respected for doing so.

- **Loyalty and the importance of standing together.**

In the late 1990s and early 2000s, I was executive chairman of Tidal Software. Tidal was a slow-growing job-scheduling software company until I brought in Thomas Charlton, first as VP of sales, then promoted him to CEO. Thomas accelerated the growth of Tidal dramatically and singlehandedly put the company on a path to success. I personally invested a lot of time in Thomas's growth, since it was his first CEO position. He repaid that investment by performing exceptionally well and listening to everything I told him. He and I had breakfast every Saturday morning to go over what had happened in the prior week and what were the plans for the coming week. Thomas and I developed a strong friendship and loyalty to each other during that time. After three years under his leadership, the revenue grew by a factor of more than five times. About that time, a larger company approached us and made overtures to acquire Tidal. As we worked through the discussions and negotiations, attempting to put together an acceptable deal, the VC companies who invested in Tidal put together an incentive package for Thomas and me to close the acquisition and supposedly compensate us for the dramatic growth. To say the incentive package was insulting was an understatement, especially considering the company was close to being worthless when Thomas and I got involved and the investors stood to make several times their investment. After seeing their offer, I told them what I thought of it. As was frequently the case, when partners in VC firms during that era were challenged, fragile egos took over and I was fired.

Thomas told me about a conversation he had with his father, Bob Charlton, when he told him I had been fired. Mr. Charlton said, "Well Thomas, you know what you have to do now, don't you? You need to decide where your loyalties lie and act accordingly."

The board put a full court press on Thomas to remain with Tidal. I encouraged Thomas to not react to my firing, but do what was in his best interest. Two days after my firing, Thomas, his VP of marketing, and his VP of sales all resigned.

Thomas and his team and I would have remained friends even if they had not resigned, but their loyalty and show of commitment is something I will never forget.

- **There may be a time when something inside you tells you it is time to make a change in your life. Listen to that voice.**

In the early 1970s, I was living in Alabama where I was born. I was attending Auburn University and working nights in the data center for a local bank. Typically, I got off work around 1:00 or 2:00 a.m., slept for a few hours, and was still able to go to school a full day.

On a Wednesday night in June, after getting home from work, I suddenly had an overpowering urge to leave Alabama and go to California. This was not a persistent dream or thought I'd ever had. When I had gotten up that morning, I had no thoughts about leaving.

My desire to leave was so great that I couldn't sleep. After a few minutes, that desire turned into determination. So at 3:00 a.m. I got up and made a list of what I would take with me and started packing the items in my backpack. The next day, Thursday, I sold my car and gave away everything that wasn't in my backpack. On Friday, I quit my job, said good-bye to my friends and family, tied my backpack and sleeping bag on my motorcycle, and left for California. That was almost fifty years ago, and I've never looked back.

I don't even want to think of how different my life would have been had I not listened to that voice.

- **What appears at the time to be an insignificant event or encounter can change the direction of your life.**

I was twenty-two years old when I left Alabama to go to California. I left so suddenly that my destination was just California. I knew, of course, that it was a big state and eventually I'd need to decide where in California I was going. My initial thinking was I'd probably go to Los Angeles, but that was because of watching TV and movies. I had actually never been there.

I had been traveling for three days when I stopped for gas outside of Phoenix, Arizona. This was back when there were service-station attendants who pumped your gas. A young boy around fourteen years old came out and was filling my tank. Seeing my backpack, bedroll, and Alabama license plate, he asked where I was going. I said "I'm going to California." "Where in California?" he asked. "Probably LA, but I haven't decided for sure," I replied. The young boy said, "LA is kind of crazy with tons of traffic all the time. Since you're from Alabama, you'd probably like San Francisco better. It's more laid-back and people are friendly." I paused for a few seconds and replied, "I never thought of that, maybe I will try San Francisco."

From that moment, my destination became San Francisco. That was almost fifty years ago, and San Francisco is still my home today.

I never knew that young boy's name or anything about him, but I've often thought how grateful I am that kid had never been to Fresno.

- **Time is going to pass either way ... so why not tackle the hard stuff**

When my oldest daughter D'Anne was getting ready to go to college, she was thinking about her major and what career she wanted to pursue. One of the considerations was a career in medicine. Like many nineteen year olds about to head off to college, she was concerned about how difficult her choice of a major would be. In a conversation with her about this, I said, "D'Anne, time is going to go by either way, so why not tackle the hard stuff?"

Today D'Anne has bachelor of arts degree in American Studies, an RN degree, a bachelor of science in nursing, a masters of science in nursing, and is a successful pediatric primary care nurse practitioner.

She tackled the hard stuff!

- **If you are going to bet on something, only bet when you know you are right. Never bet because you think someone else is wrong.**

One of the best sales reps I've ever worked with is Patricia Foerster. I've worked with her twice, first at XA Systems, then again at Unison Software.

At XA, I had just assigned Hawaii as one of the states in Patricia's territory when I asked her about a particular account. She said she had tried to call them and was planning a follow-up call the next day when the conversation turned to the time difference between California and Hawaii. I commented that since it was winter and California was on Pacific Standard Time there was only a two-hour time difference between California and Hawaii. Patricia strongly objected and said, "Oh no, there is more than a two-hour difference!" I asked "How many hours time difference do you think there is?" She said, "I'm not sure, but I know it's more than two." I said, "Well, right now there is only a two-hour difference."

She quickly responded with, "I'll bet you $100 that it is more than two!" I took her bet.

I then asked another friend who was observing the exchange to call the Hawaii Hilton Village Hotel in Honolulu and ask what time it is there. Then from memory, I gave him the phone number for the hotel. Our friend looked at Patricia and said, "I think you're in trouble." I was right, of course. I had been to Hawaii more than twenty-five times.

I did take Patricia's money, but I bought her a clock with a time zone dial that cost $100. That took place took place more than twenty-five years ago, and she still has that clock sitting on her desk.

- **Never argue with a dumbass.**

When you find yourself interacting with someone whose logic and ideas are not well thought out or whose opinions were formed with no basis in sound intellectual insight, leave them to their world and don't waste time trying to convince them there may be other points of view to consider. Your attempts will almost always fail. Arguing with such people is a futile effort.

Although some may read this and find my words unkind or feel I am speaking down to those I find less informed, that's not what I am doing.

The fact is, there are people with ideas, beliefs, and interpretations that are so far off base that no one will ever get through to them. Too often, I've seen others engage in arguments and debates that quickly go from bad to worse. If you do that you are in effect lowering yourself to their level. Don't be tempted to do that. It's far better to just smile, nod, and leave.

- **Never give up on yourself.**

My first job out of college was with the San Francisco office of SBC, a computer and timesharing company. Timesharing was a market segment that was the forerunner to the software industry. SBC had been a division of IBM, and still had a strong pin-stripe-suit, white-shirt, and wingtips culture. They had an extensive training program for all new hires that ran for six months. We attended three separate training sessions in Tarrytown, New York, that were so intense a significant number of new hires were gone by the end of the six-month program.

When I got the offer, I launched into the job with everything I had. I worked harder than ever and was determined to succeed. There were five or six other trainees hired in the San Francisco office at the same time, and we went through training together. I was fearless and dared anyone to outwork me.

SBC had monthly phone days when everyone was in the office calling prospects and scheduling appointments. That was before voicemail, so when you called someone, eventually a live person answered the phone. The full-quota sales reps would give us trainees a list of some of their prospects and allow us to attempt to schedule appointments for them. As part of our training, they took us along on the calls we scheduled. During my first phone day, I was given a list of around fifty companies to call. I did extensive research and preparation and started the day early, ready to go. At the end of the day, I had scheduled thirty-five appointments, more than anyone in the office, quota reps included. The rep who came in second had ten.

That day helped set the expectations for my sales career. I continued to work hard and excel at every task I was given and every training session I attended. My six-month training period ended in June and I was placed on quota and given a territory of thirty San Francisco Bay-area companies to sell to. None were current customers. It was a raw, prospecting territory.

To say it was a tough assignment was an understatement. Sales into the companies I was given had been attempted numerous times without success. Trying to make progress in accounts where several before me had failed was difficult, and I found myself getting really discouraged. No one seemed that interested in our products, and most didn't want to meet with me. I started questioning if I had made the right decision choosing a career in sales.

One morning in early July, I had an appointment with one of my accounts at 10:00 a.m. I didn't go into my office before the appointment, instead I drove directly to the prospect's office building, got there at 8:30, and sat in my car in the parking lot until 10:00.

When 10:00 came, instead of going inside for the appointment, I started my car and drove home. I sat at home for the next few hours feeling worse with every minute, filled with self-doubt, and convinced that I was a failure in sales.

At 3:00 p.m., I drove to the office and went in to see my sales manager, Jack Riley. Jack was one of the best salesmen I've ever known. I walked into his office, sat down, and told him what I had done. I said I had come to the realization that I was not cut out for sales and had decided to quit and find another career.

Jack was an unusual guy and had some, for lack of a better word, quirky habits. He would sometimes stare at the ceiling while you were talking to him, or play with a pen or pencil during a conversation. On this particular day, while I was crying and pouring my heart out, Jack was leaning back in his chair looking at the ceiling balancing a pencil between his upper lip and his nose. But I knew he was listening.

When I finished telling my story, Jack dropped the pencil and leaned forward across his desk toward me. He looked me straight in the eye and said, "Congratulations! You have just figured out something that most salesmen don't figure out for years. You figured out that if you are not prepared, don't have a good plan, and don't stay ahead of it, this job will eat you alive!" He went on to say that for me to say I'm not cut out for sales is ridiculous. He said, "You have sales skills running out of your ears!" He then told me to go get all of my account folders and bring them to his office and together we were going to build me a territory plan that would put me at the top.

We stayed in the office until after 8:00 p.m. working on my territory plan. By the time I left, I was walking on air. The change in my attitude and feeling about my future was nothing short of astounding.

That was July. The full-year quota for key new accounts for a full-quota rep was four. From July through December that year, I closed nine key new accounts, more than anyone in the country closed during that six-month period.

That turnaround came about because someone believed in me and would not let me give up on myself. Who knows what would have happened if I had been working for someone less caring and less talented than Jack Riley. But fortunately for me, that's who I was working for. I have always known that I owe him a great deal of gratitude.

Unfortunately, Jack passed away in 1998. The last time I saw him we met for lunch in the fall of 1997 for me to congratulate him on entering the *Guinness Book of World Records*. He had completed fifty-two triathlons in one calendar year.

Thank you, Jack, for believing in me and not allowing me to give up on myself.

- **It is a proven fact that almost anyone can be taught to sell. But some people are born with traits that give them a big head start.**

When my stepson Mehron was in college, he took a part-time job going door to door, selling new windows to home-owners. These were knocking-on-doors, cold-call sales, not following up on previously scheduled appointments. Door-to-door selling is one of the most difficult sales jobs there is. But Mehron excelled at it. He was fearless, confident, and a tireless worker.

When he graduated from college, I convinced him to come to work for my company and join our telesales team. I knew that if he could succeed at selling windows door to door he would have no trouble selling software to businesses.

He completed his rookie year as the top salesman in the company and has not slowed down since.

- **One man with courage makes a majority.**

When one person steps up and takes control of a chaotic situation by laying out a coherent plan, showing leadership, fearless determination, and a focused drive toward a set of goals, rarely if ever will they be challenged.

During a long and exhaustive European road trip with my colleague and good friend Phil Sheridan, we were dealing with frustrating interference and inconsistent directions from our headquarters when I came to the conclusion that the only way we were going to accomplish what we had set out to do was for me to ignore the interference, take control of the situation, do what needed to be done, and let the chips fall where they may.

At the end of one of those frustrating days, at dinner Phil handed me a sheet of paper from his notepad with the words, "One man with courage makes a majority" written on it. That was more than thirty years ago. I carried that note folded in my rolling to-do journals for twenty years and still have it today.

It was the perfect inspiration then, and still is.

- **The wisdom of children.**

I have four daughters, and have been taking them with me on business trips around the U.S. and Europe starting when they were six or seven years old. When I had a meeting with someone, I took the one who was travelling with me to the meeting and explained to whoever I was seeing that my daughter was traveling with me. She would sit quietly and either read or entertain herself with a game.

My counterpart was almost always a man near my age who often had children of his own. Talk about an icebreaker, rapport builder, or making yourself memorable, try taking your beautiful young daughter to a business meeting. I was often a distraction to them talking to and entertaining my daughter. Not once was that even a hint of an issue. I had business associates years later still asking me about my daughters.

When my daughter Jennifer was about eight years old, I took her on a trip to San Diego. We arrived just after lunch and took the afternoon to visit some of the attractions in the area. As we were driving around, Jennifer asked me. "Dad, how do you know your way around San Diego so well?" I said, "I come here often for business meetings." She asked, "What do you do in business meetings?" "We talk," I said. She asked, "Is that all you do, just talk?" I said, "Yes, that's all we do." She thought for a minute then asked, "Dad, you ever heard of a telephone?"

- **A certain level of sophistication can make you memorable.**

Juli, my youngest daughter, was ten years old when she and I went to Newport Beach, California, for a combination business trip and daddy-daughter weekend getaway. We stayed at the Balboa Beach Club and had several fun activities on Saturday. On Saturday evening, we went to the restaurant at the club for dinner.

The captain seated us, and asked if we would like any appetizers before dinner. Juli looked at the menu and saw they served caviar. She was familiar with it and amazingly, for a ten year old, loved it and asked if we could have some. I said sure.

A few minutes later, the captain brought a service of caviar and laid it out on our table. Juli noticed there was no crème fraîche, so she asked, "Do you have crème fraîche?" The captain nodded and said, "Certainly."

A couple of minutes later, he came back with a small bowl with what appeared to be crème fraîche. After tasting it, Juli said, "I don't think this is crème fraîche. It tastes like sour cream."

The captain looked at me and said, "Mr Edwards, I assume this is your daughter." I smiled and said, "Yes, this is my daughter." He smiled back and nodded, then said, "Good luck, Sir!"

For many years after, every time I had dinner at the club the captain would ask about Juli and recall fondly the level of sophistication of a ten year old girl, often sharing the experience with others neadby.

• **Education → Experience → Knowledge → Judgment → Wisdom**

Learning, growing, achievement, and success is a lifelong process and involves many steps, stops, and starts.

Here is one summary of that process.

Education

Education is the first step you must take. In many countries, it is essentially free. Anyone who says they can't afford an education needs to re-assess their priorities.

Experience

With education comes the opportunity to get a job and gain experience.

Knowledge

After years of working, you acquire knowledge, the kind that only comes from experience.

Judgment

After decades of education, experience, and acquiring knowledge, you may develop the ability to exercise judgment.

Wisdom

Wisdom is not guaranteed. It does not come to everyone, only to those few who, after many years, have the ability to see more than others see when looking at the same situation. They make connections and anticipate reactions that are not apparent to other people. If you are fortunate enough to know someone blessed with wisdom, cherish them and hold on to that relationship.